理工类学术论文英语写作与发表指南

李义宝 编著　金俊石（Junseok KIM）主审

西安交通大学出版社
XI'AN JIAOTONG UNIVERSITY PRESS

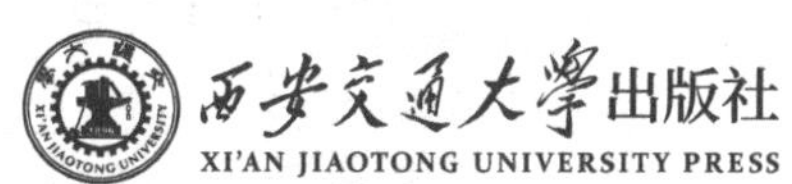

图书在版编目(CIP)数据

理工类学术论文英语写作与发表指南 / 李义宝编著. 西安 ：西安交通大学出版社，2024. 7. -- ISBN 978-7-5693-2770-0

Ⅰ. H315-62

中国国家版本馆 CIP 数据核字第 2024B6A976 号

理工类学术论文英语写作与发表指南

LIGONGLEI XUESHU LUNWEN YINGYU XIEZUO YU FABIAO ZHINAN

编　　著　李义宝
责任编辑　蔡乐芊
责任校对　庞钧颖
封面设计　伍　胜

出版发行　西安交通大学出版社
（西安市兴庆南路 1 号　邮政编码 710048）
网　　址　http://www.xjtupress.com
电　　话　(029)82668357　82667874(市场营销中心)
(029)82668315(总编办)
传　　真　(029)82668280
印　　刷　西安五星印刷有限公司

开　　本　720 mm×1000 mm　1/16　**印张**　7.875　**字数**　126 千字
版次印次　2024 年 7 月第 1 版　2024 年 7 月第 1 次印刷
书　　号　ISBN 978-7-5693-2770-0
定　　价　45.00 元

如发现印装质量问题，请与本社市场营销中心联系调换。
订购热线：(029)82668851　82668852
投稿热线：(029)82665371

目　录

CONTENTS

1 给青年学者的一些建议

研究论文是研究人员展示本人科学研究成果的重要载体之一。研究论文的写作目的是与他人分享和交流研究成果，需要以特定格式提交，经过同行评审之后，才可以正式发表。研究论文的写作是一项复杂的工程。

我也是一名科研工作者。我结合个人的经历，总结了一些对青年学者的建议，希望有所帮助。

• 在科学研究方面，您需认真执行导师的要求并积极参与研究项目。通过协助撰写研究计划书、联合撰写研究论文以及规划资助费用等工作，您会锻炼独立撰写研究提案和研究论文的能力。这将为您后续研究工作的顺利开展奠定基础。

• 选择了开启学术研究之门，就意味着研究压力的开始。您必须有足够的积累才能产出研究成果。研究成果的一个重要形式就是论文。

• 即使您不是论文的主要作者，您都应该以负责任的方式认真思考研究内容，并尽最大努力撰写论文。如果因为您不是主要作者或通讯作者就轻视写论文的过程，那么您学到的东西将很有限。

• 在与其他学者共同撰写论文时，必须尽最大努力为论文作出贡献，直至论文完成。联合研究能够通过结合不同领域的专业知识来发挥协同效应。此外，通过对其他研究人员提出问题并交流学习，您可以获取新的知识。

- 不要吝啬与您一同走在学术道路上的人分享知识。您应该发自内心地与他们分享和交流，永远不要采取傲慢的态度。可能在您以后需要帮助的时候，他们也会伸出援手。

- 不要舍不得购买复印纸、打印机、墨水和碳粉。相关的参考论文需要被打印出来才能方便阅读。此外，正在撰写的论文草稿也需要打印出来才会方便查看和更正错误。要清楚地认识到即使用掉 1 盒 A4 纸和 1 盒碳粉来完成一篇论文，那也不是浪费金钱。

- 多接触沉浸在学习中的学者。对于年轻学者来说，最重要的是找到可以成为自己榜样的老师、前辈、同事甚至后辈。当您不知道该怎么做时，试试多接触沉浸在学习中的学者，事实证明这是很有效的。

- 积极参加各类学术活动。学校或研究所的部门公告板上经常会张贴学术研讨会信息。几乎所有的研讨会都欢迎感兴趣的人来试听。研讨会结束后如果能和主讲人一起共进晚餐，那将是很难得的一次深入交流的机会。

- 从好的演讲中总结技巧并汲取最佳实践经验，将其作为自己演讲的模板。当听到不尽如人意的演讲时，要分析原因，并尽量避免自己出现类似情况。建议硕士期间主要进行海报展示，博士期间进行口头报告。尽可能在会议开始前作好准备。在会议期间，仔细听您感兴趣的演讲报告，扩充您的知识储备。

- 如果您有感兴趣的研讨会主题，请提前阅读与研讨会主题相关的论文。这样可以在研讨会期间有针对性地对不了解的部分提出问题。如果有可能的话，请参加研讨会的晚宴并提出更详细的问题，这样可以在短时间内获得更多知识。幸运的话，您甚至可能会找到新的研究课题。

- 即使提交给会议的论文没有发表，感到沮丧的时间不要太久，最好不要超过一天。要求苛刻的期刊的退稿率会超过 60%。作为青年学者，被拒稿是很正常的。尽管如此，您也需要认真准备您的论文，同时客观地看待审稿人的意见，不厌其烦地修改。

- 当论文写到一定程度时，需要收集并学习相关论文，好好利用其中好的表达方式。

- 可将参考文献按字段放在 PDF 文件中。PDF 文件的名称应与论文题目一致，以便查阅时尽快地了解参考论文的内容。当收集到一定数量的参考论文时，将它们按主题打印、装订、存储，以便在需要时系统阅读和引用。

- 在购买新书前，可以先阅读基本内容，对它有一个整体了解。不要因为书名比较有吸引力，就贸然购买这本书。要找到与自己研究领域相关的参考书籍。

- 当科研上有新的想法时，应该立即进行实践和验证。否则随着时间的推移，这个好的想法会被遗忘。

- 研究生应该在学习上多投入一些时间。要处理好社会活动与学习的关系，把主要精力放在科研上。

- 不要害怕超过您的指导老师。著名运动员往往比他们的教练有更多的技巧和更强的能力。努力投入研究会使您的导师感到高兴和欣慰。

- 抄袭是学者的致命污点。论文一经发表将永存在学术界，如果有抄袭成分，终有一天抄袭的事实会被别人发现。在写作过程中应该仔细审查您写的论文，以避免抄袭。

2 基本信息

本章首先介绍了谷歌学术(Google Scholar)、SCOPUS 数据库和科学引文索引(SCI 和 SCIE)等检索库的特点及使用,然后介绍了影响因子(IF)的定义和按影响因子排名对目标领域的文献如何进行检索、获取被引次数的方法及国际标准期刊号(ISSN)等基本知识。

2.1 谷歌学术

您可以输入与研究主题有关的关键字在谷歌学术(http://scholar.google.com)中查找相关论文,一般默认搜索结果按引用次数从大到小排序。当您想检索最新发表的论文时,可以从页面左侧的菜单中选择需要的年份,从所选年份至今已发表的论文列表就会在页面上显示出来。如果要引用检索到的论文,您可以单击"引用"按钮,然后复制论文信息。此外,检索时如果想缩小范围,可把搜索内容放在双引号中,这样检索出来的内容仅显示双引号中的内容结果。

2.2 SCOPUS 数据库

SCOPUS 数据库(http://www.info.scopus.com)是爱思唯尔出版社(Elsevier)提供的摘要和引文数据库,可以为读者提供学术期刊、参考文献、引文索引等信息，其论文更新会快于其他网站。

2.3 科学引文索引

SCI 和 SCIE 均为科学引文索引，涉及数、理、化、农、医等多个学例。它不仅是一种大型的文献检索工具，还是引文分析的重要工具。2020 年，考虑到 SCI 和 SCIE 在选刊标准上已经没有区别，科瑞唯安(Clarivate Analytice)决定不再使用 SCI 的叫法，统一称为 SCIE 收录文章。

2.4 获取被引次数

在谷歌学术中，“cited by”表示引用次数，其中还包括对会议报告和非正式文章的引用情况统计。而汤森路透(Thomson Reuters)的 Web of Knowledge (http://apps. webofknowledge. com/)则显示对官方学术论文的引用。Web of Science 是科睿唯安旗下的全球引文数据库。在 Web of Science 下的空白处输入论文的标题、作者或期刊名称，单击“检索”即可查看检索结果。如果单击“主题”然后检索，则会显示与检索词相对应的文章；继续单击搜索出的论文，页面则会出现标题、作者和期刊名称、文章摘要以及引用次数(被引频次)等结果，如图 2-1 所示。图 2-1 是标题为 A Nonlinear Convex Splitting Fourier Spectral Scheme for the Cahn-Hilliard Equation with a Logarithmic Free Energy 的论文搜索结果。点击期刊信息中的影响因子，在出现的期刊引文报告中就会显示该期刊的影响因子。影响因子是指为期刊计算的指数，引用次数指的是单个论文的引用次数。

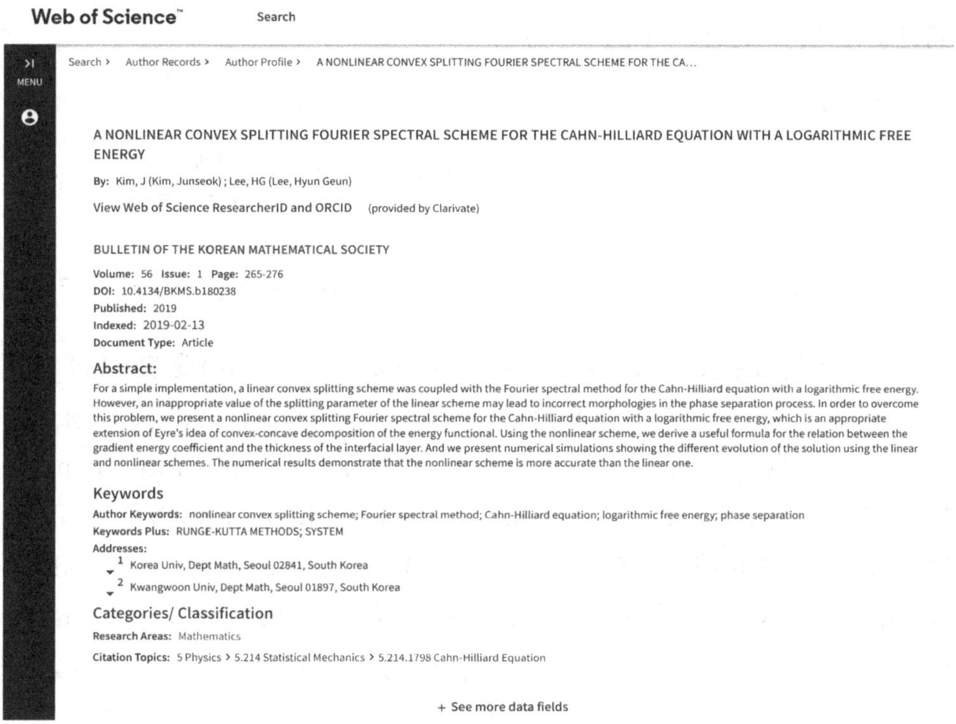

Web of Science™ Search

Search › Author Records › Author Profile › A NONLINEAR CONVEX SPLITTING FOURIER SPECTRAL SCHEME FOR THE CA...

MENU

A NONLINEAR CONVEX SPLITTING FOURIER SPECTRAL SCHEME FOR THE CAHN-HILLIARD EQUATION WITH A LOGARITHMIC FREE ENERGY

By: Kim, J (Kim, Junseok) ; Lee, HG (Lee, Hyun Geun)

View Web of Science ResearcherID and ORCID (provided by Clarivate)

BULLETIN OF THE KOREAN MATHEMATICAL SOCIETY

Volume: 56 Issue: 1 Page: 265-276
DOI: 10.4134/BKMS.b180238
Published: 2019
Indexed: 2019-02-13
Document Type: Article

Abstract:

For a simple implementation, a linear convex splitting scheme was coupled with the Fourier spectral method for the Cahn-Hilliard equation with a logarithmic free energy. However, an inappropriate value of the splitting parameter of the linear scheme may lead to incorrect morphologies in the phase separation process. In order to overcome this problem, we present a nonlinear convex splitting Fourier spectral scheme for the Cahn-Hilliard equation with a logarithmic free energy, which is an appropriate extension of Eyre's idea of convex-concave decomposition of the energy functional. Using the nonlinear scheme, we derive a useful formula for the relation between the gradient energy coefficient and the thickness of the interfacial layer. And we present numerical simulations showing the different evolution of the solution using the linear and nonlinear schemes. The numerical results demonstrate that the nonlinear scheme is more accurate than the linear one.

Keywords

Author Keywords: nonlinear convex splitting scheme; Fourier spectral method; Cahn-Hilliard equation; logarithmic free energy; phase separation
Keywords Plus: RUNGE-KUTTA METHODS; SYSTEM
Addresses:
1 Korea Univ, Dept Math, Seoul 02841, South Korea
2 Kwangwoon Univ, Dept Math, Seoul 01897, South Korea

Categories/ Classification

Research Areas: Mathematics
Citation Topics: 5 Physics › 5.214 Statistical Mechanics › 5.214.1798 Cahn-Hilliard Equation

+ See more data fields

图 2－1 Web of Science 上论文的详细信息以及被引次数

2.5 影响因子及影响因子排名

影响因子(Impact Factor，IF)指期刊的影响力指数。它通过计算期刊上发表论文的引用次数得出,其计算方法如下:

某期刊 x 年的影响因子为

$$\frac{(x-1)\text{年和}(x-2)\text{年总计发表的论文在 }x\text{ 年被引用次数}}{(x-1)\text{年和}(x-2)\text{年总计发表的论文数量}}$$

图 2 - 2 是《计算物理学》期刊(*Journal of Computational Physics*)2021 年影响因子。在 2019 年已发表的论文中,2021 年被引用次数为 3515 ;在 2020 年发表的论文中,2021 年被引用次数为 2737。因此,两年的总被引次数为 6252 。此外,该期刊 2019 年发表的论文数量为 667 篇,2020 年发表的论文数量 679 篇,共 1346 篇。代

入上述影响因子计算公式，得出该刊 2021 年 IF＝6252/1346＝4.645。同理计算出其最近 5 年的 IF 为 3.948。

CiteScore 2021

7.1 = 18,653 引文 2018 - 2021 / 2,644 篇文献 2018 - 2021

于 05 May, 2022 计算

CiteScoreTracker 2022

7.8 = 到目前为止 21,570 次引用 / 到目前为止 2,766 篇文献

最近更新于 05 March, 2023 • 按月更新

图 2－2 《计算物理学》(*Journal of Computational Physics*)的影响因子计算

《期刊引证报告》(Journal Citation Reports，JCR)是美国科学信息研究所(ISI)出版的对期刊进行全面评估的资源工具。其数据来自美国科学信息研究所的五个引文索引数据库：Science Citation Index-Expanded (SCIE)、Social Sciences Citation Index(SSCI)、Arts & Humanities Citation Index (ACHCI)、Conference Proceedings Citation Index-Science 以及 Conference Proceedings Citation Index-Social Science & Humanities。各期刊的引文统计信息自 1975 年以来每年更新一次。

研究人员可以在 Web of Science 官网上查询期刊影响因子的排名。在 Master Search 字段中输入期刊名称，并选择按年份搜索期刊的影响因子。点击底部的排名就会显示期刊按类别的排名，例如 26/105 表示在该领域有 105 种期刊，搜索期刊排名第 26 位。另外，它还可能属于其他领域，例如在其他领域是 3/55，表示其他领域有 55 种期刊，该刊排名第 3。3/55×100％的计算结果为 5.45％，表示该期刊为该领域排名为前 5.45％ 的期刊。

《期刊引证报告》根据影响因子将期刊分为四个等级(四分位排名)：排名前 25％的期刊属于 Q1 区；排名 25％到 50％的期刊属于 Q2 区；排名 50％到 75％的期刊属于 Q3 区；剩下的则属于 Q4 区。

《中国科学院文献情报中心期刊分区表》对 SCIE、SSCI 和 A&HCI 全部期刊进行分区，最终划分出四个分区。分区表包括大类分区和小类分区：大类分区是将期刊按照自定义的 13 个学科所做的分区。而小类分区是将期刊按照《期刊引证报告》已有学科分类体系所做的分区。查询网址为：http://www.fenqubiao.com/。查询方法请参考图 2－3。

期刊全称：	COMPUTER METHODS IN APPLIED MECHANICS AND ENGINEERING		
期刊简称：	COMPUT METHOD APPL M	ISSN：	0045-7825
年份：	2021年	综述：	否

	学科名称	分区	Top期刊
小类	ENGINEERING, MULTIDISCIPLINARY工程：综合	1	-
小类	MATHEMATICS, INTERDISCIPLINARY APPLICATIONS数学跨学科应用	1	-
小类	MECHANICS力学	1	-
大类	工程技术	2	是

期刊影响因子				总被引频次		
2018年	2019年	2020年	2018-2020年平均	2019年	2020年	2019年-2020年
4.821	5.763	6.756	5.780	33874	40986	74860

图 2－3　中科院文献情报中心期刊分区查询方式

2.6　数字对象唯一标识符

DOI (Digital Object Identifier)是数字对象唯一标识符，如同文献的身份证号码，具有唯一性和永久性。您可以通过访问网站 http://www.crossref.org/guestquery 查找论文的 DOI。

详细方法请参考下列图示（图 2－4 至图 2－7）。

Crossref

free DOI lookup

Crossref currently provides a number of ways for you to locate a DOI.

- If you have bibliographic data for a item and would like to find the DOI, please use the metadata section of this form.
- If you only have an article title and author, please use the article title search section of this form.
- If you have the text of a bibliographic reference, please use our Simple Text Query service.
- If you are a developer and wish to submit a raw XML query use the XML form section of this page.

Bibliographic metadata search

This form is a guest query interface to the Crossref system for individual DOI retrieval. This interface is not intended for automated querying. If you would like to query Crossref on an automated batch basis, please obtain an account on our system.

You must supply either author or first page and we recommend using journal title as well as ISSN. For a list of journal titles in the Crossref holdings please visit our browsable journal list.

Limit search to: ◉ Journal OR ○ Book/Conference Proceeding

First Author ISSN

Journal Title

Article Title

Volume Issue Page Year

ISBN Component Number

Series Title

Enable Multiple Hits ☑

Search Clear Form

Search on article title

If you only know the title of an item (article, book chapter, report, working-paper ... etc.) and the author submit them here. This form is a guest query interface to the Crossref system for individual DOI retrieval. This interface is not intended for automated querying. If you would like to query Crossref on an automated batch basis, please obtain an account on our system.

First Author (surname)

Article Title

Enable Multiple Hits ☑

Search Clear Form

A DOI query

Select result format -- xml-xsd: ◉ OR unixref: ○

DOI:

Search

Build an XML query (click here) (for experts only!)

You may enter a query in XML form if you know the tags and wish to experiment with the query control attributes.

图 2－4 http://www.crossref.org/guestquery 网站首页

Search on article title

If you only know the title of an item (article, book chapter, report, working-paper ... etc.) and the author submit them here. This form is a guest query interface to the Crossref system for individual DOI retrieval. This interface is not intended for automated querying. If you would like to query Crossref on an automated batch basis, please obtain an account on our system.

First Author (surname): Li

Article Title: An efficient and stable compact fourth-order finite difference scheme for the phase field crystal equation

Enable Multiple Hits: ☑

Search | Clear Form

Journal Title	Author	ISSN	Volume	Issue	Page	Year
Persistent Link						
Article Title						
Computer Methods in Applied Mechanics and Engineering	Li	00457825	319		194	2017
http://dx.doi.org/10.1016/j.cma.2017.02.022						
An efficient and stable compact fourth-order finite difference scheme for the phase field crystal equation						

图 2－5　输入作者姓氏和论文题目，然后点击搜索按钮

Search on article title

If you only know the title of an item (article, book chapter, report, working-paper ... etc.) and the author submit them here. This form is a guest query interface to the Crossref system for individual DOI retrieval. This interface is not intended for automated querying. If you would like to query Crossref on an automated batch basis, please obtain an account on our system.

First Author (surname): Li

Article Title: An efficient and stable compact fourth-order finite difference scheme for the phase field crystal equation

Enable Multiple Hits: ☑

Search | Clear Form

Journal Title	Author	ISSN	Volume	Issue	Page	Year
Persistent Link						
Article Title						
Computer Methods in Applied Mechanics and Engineering	Li	00457825	319		194	2017
http://dx.doi.org/10.1016/j.cma.2017.02.022						
An efficient and stable compact fourth-order finite difference scheme for the phase field crystal equation						

图 2－6　论文 DOI 显示结果

An efficient and stable compact fourth-order finite difference scheme for the phase field crystal equation

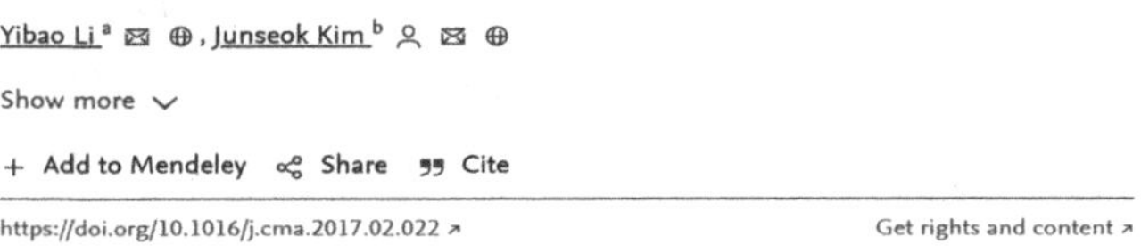

图 2－7　单击论文 DOI 可以找到更多信息

3 科技论文写作

3.1 论文主题的选择

一篇好的学术论文应该具有独创性。论文的研究主题应是新颖有趣的而且是最具有挑战性的。论文应针对学术界关注的难点和热点问题，提出相应的解决方案。具体来说，可以通过以下途径和方法激发灵感。

- 从最近发表的论文或有关研究主题的结论中获取想法。
- 对于现有方法无法解决的问题，尝试换一种新的解决方案。
- 揭示现有分析的局限性，并提出解决这些局限性的新方法。
- 虽然可以从其他研究人员的学术论文中获得论文的研究方向和主题，但论文的发表一般需要几个月或几年的时间。因此为了尽快地确定论文题目，可以通过研讨会等了解最新的研究趋势，尤其是通过向演讲者提问来得到更深层次的理解。
- 如果你是研究生，并且导师可以确定论文的主题，那么你可以在导师的严格指导下撰写论文。

需要注意的是，选择论文主题时要谨慎。你需要考虑论文主题是否与要投稿的期刊相契合，否则可能会浪费时间。

确定论文选题后，接下来就要考虑论文的架构，并开始准备撰写论文。撰写论文时应简明扼要，充分考虑读者的阅读需求，同时应详述必要数据和操作过程，以便读者可以复现实验结果，最后应规范引用参考文献。以下是应用数值分析领域论文的结构示例参考。

Title
Abstract
Introduction
Governing equations
Numerical method
Numerical results
Conclusions
Statements and Declarations
Acknowledgments
Appendix
References

撰写论文时，要不停思考、修改标题、引言、正文、结果、结论等内容，使它们在逻辑上能够有机地联系起来。接下来，我们将详细讨论各部分的撰写原则和方法。

3.2 论文标题的确定

标题在论文的最前面，是读者最先看到的内容，会很大程度上影响读者是否愿意继续阅读论文。因此，标题应该尽可能准确地概括和解释论文内容，应表明论文的主题和目的，好的论文标题要能够吸引读者，让读者有兴趣深入了解论文的研究主题。另外，论文标题应以尽可能少的字数简明扼要地表达主题，但不应太短，以免造成读者理解困难。例如 Studies on Brucella 这样的标题太短，很难让读者了解论文的内容是什么。On the addition to the method of microscopic research by a new way of producing colour-contrast between an object and its background or between definite parts of the object itself 这个题目又太长，读者很难理解其表达的内容。

3.2.1 标题格式

标题中单词大小写的书写规则可能因期刊而异，请以投稿期刊的格式为准。

- An Unconditionally Gradient Stable Adaptive Mesh Refinement for the Cahn-Hilliard Equation（每一个单词的首字母大写）
- An unconditionally gradient stable numerical method for solving the Allen-Cahn equation（除专有名词外，仅第一个单词的首字母大写）
- NUMERICAL METHODS FOR FOURTH ORDER NONLINEAR DEGENERATE DIFFUSION PROBLEMS（所有单词都大写）

3.2.2 副标题

副标题通常用来更具体地描述研究主题，引导读者对文章内容有更深入的了解。一般用冒号连接标题和副标题。具体例子如下。

- Finite element methods for Navier-Stokes equations：theory and algorithms
- ON ERROR ESTIMATES OF PROJECTION METHODS FOR NAVIER-STOKES EQUATIONS：FIRST-ORDER SCHEMES

3.2.3 栏外标题

写作时您可以通过在论文的奇数页或偶数页的顶部附加一个简短的栏外标题(Running title)来指示论文的特征。在这里，论文题目被进一步压缩，长度一般为 50～60 个字符，具体长度要以投稿期刊的规定为准。

3.2.4 标题写作的注意事项

- 论文标题中尽量不要出现缩写、数学符号和公式。
- 在包含研究人员姓名的模型、方程或方法中不要使用定冠词 the，比如：Chan-Vese model、Cahn-Hilliard model。
- 尽量不要使用 new 这个单词。因为 10 年或 20 年后，即使论文的题目中含有 new 这个单词，但内容也可能不是新的了。
- 标题应尽量避免以 A study of 此类表述开头。

3.2.5 标题示例

以下是一些论文标题的示例。

- A second-order projection method for the incompressible Navier-Stokes equations
- On the interior regularity of weak solutions of the Navier-Stokes equations
- On the convergence of discrete approximations to the Navier-Stokes equations
- On the time-dependent solution of the incompressible Navier-Stokes equations in two and three dimensions
- A multiphase level set framework for image segmentation using the Mumford and Shah model
- A front-tracking method for the computations of multiphase flow
- A comparison study of the conservative Allen-Cahn and Cahn-Hilliard equations

论文标题应该能够恰当地概括论文的内容。写完论文后，请再回顾一下论文的主旨是什么，主要贡献是什么，论文题目是否准确地总结了论文内容。必要的话，请继续修改标题直到找到一个最合适的。

3.3 作者及单位署名

3.3.1 作者署名

论文作者署名最好始终使用作者的英文姓名，因为在搜索引擎（如 MathSciNet）中按作者姓名搜索时，如果作者姓名的语言不同，该作者的所有论文一般在列表中不会全部出现。另外，应该遵守期刊的署名规则。有的期刊要求按照作者姓氏的字母顺序排序。一般情况下，应与通讯作者或责任作者协商决定作者姓名顺序。

3.3.2 单位署名

隶属关系应遵循投稿期刊的格式要求，例如：School of Mathematics and Statistics, Xi'an Jiaotong University, Xi'an 710049, China。

3.4 摘要和关键词

3.4.1 摘要概述及示例

摘要是对论文内容精练、准确、全面的总结。因此，摘要应包括论文中主要研究结果的所有信息，使读者在不阅读正文的情况下也能了解论文主要研究成果。摘要不仅可以帮助读者快速、准确地了解论文的基本内容，而且可以帮助读者决定是否继续仔细阅读整篇文章。由于摘要的作用十分重要，而且是论文的第一部分，因此，大多数作者都会在完成正文内容之后，重点书写摘要，仔细阅读摘要中的每个句子，并反复核实正文中的内容是否被准确表达出来。摘要的长度不应超过投稿期刊的要求字数，一般来说是 150 ～ 250 字。摘要应该简洁且准确地概括以下内容：

- 研究的主要目的和研究的范围。
- 为达到研究目的所选择的方法。
- 研究的主要结果以及得出的结论。

给大家分享一个实用的方法。可以在谷歌学术或 Web of Science 中搜索大约 10 篇同类型的研究论文，只打印每篇论文的摘要页，看看有没有您需要的英文表述，并参考搜索出来的摘要来对自己的摘要进行修改和补充。同行专家对提交给期刊的论文在只阅读摘要的情况下也可以进行评审，所以摘要要写得非常准确细致。以下是已发表论文的摘要示例。

A second-order projection method for the incompressible Navier-Stokes equations [2]

Abstract: In this paper we describe a second-order projection method for the time-dependent, incompressible Navier–Stokes equations. As in the original projection method developed by Chorin, we first solve diffusion-convection equations to predict intermediate velocities which are then projected onto the space of divergence-free vector fields. By introducing more coupling between the diffusion-convection step and the projection step we obtain a temporal discretization that is second-order accurate. Our treatment of the diffusion-convection step uses a specialized higher order Godunov method for differencing the nonlinear convective terms that provides a robust treatment of these terms at high Reynolds number. The Godunov procedure is second-order accurate for smooth flow and remains stable for discontinuous initial data, even in the zero-viscosity limit. We approximate the projection directly using a Galerkin procedure that uses a local basis for discretely divergence - free vector fields.

Numerical results are presented validating the convergence properties of the method. We also apply the method to doubly periodic shear-layers to assess the performance of the method on more difficult applications.

描述本研究的主要目的和范围 → In this paper we describe a second-order projection method for the time-dependent, incompressible Navier-Stokes equations.

描述为达到研究目的所选择的方法 → As in the original projection method developed by Chorin, we first solve diffusion-convection equations to predict intermediate velocities which are then projected onto the space of divergence-free vector fields. By introducing more coupling between the diffusion-convection step and the projection step we obtain a temporal discretization that is second-order accurate. Our treatment of the diffusion-convection step uses a specialized higher order Godunov method for differencing the nonlinear convective terms that provides a robust treatment of these terms at high Reynolds number. The Godunov procedure is second-order accurate for smooth flow and remains stable for discontinuous initial data, even in the zero-viscosity limit. We approximate the projection directly using a Galerkin procedure that uses a local basis for discretely divergence-free vector fields.

简述研究结果和结论 → Numerical results are presented validating the convergence properties of the method. We also apply the method to doubly periodic shear-layers to assess the performance of the method on more difficult applications.

Application of a fractional-step method to incompressible Navier-Stokes equations [11]

Abstract: A numerical method for computing three-dimensional, time-dependent incompressible flows is presented. The method is based on a fractional-step, or time-splitting, scheme in conjunction with the approximate-factorization technique. It is shown that the use of velocity boundary conditions for the intermediate velocity field can lead to inconsistent numerical solutions. Appropriate boundary conditions for the intermediate velocity field are derived and tested. Numerical solutions for flows inside a driven cavity and over a backward-facing step are presented and compared with experimental data and other numerical results.

描述本研究的主要目的和范围 → A numerical method for computing three-dimensional, time-dependent incompressible flows is presented.

描述为达到研究目的所选择的方法 → The method is based on a fractional-step, or time-splitting, scheme in conjunction with the approximate-factorization technique. It is shown that the use of velocity boundary conditions for the intermediate velocity field can lead to inconsistent numerical solutions. Appropriate boundary conditions for the intermediate velocity field are derived and tested.

简述研究结果和结论 → Numerical solutions for flows inside a driven cavity and over a backward-facing step are presented and compared with experimental data and other numerical results.

Numerical simulations of phase separation dynamics in a water-oil-surfactant system [13]

Abstract: We have studied numerically the dynamics of the microphase separation of a water-oil-surfactant system. We developed an efficient and accurate numerical method for solving the two-dimensional time-dependent Ginzburg-Landau model with two order parameters. The numerical method is based on a conservative, second-order accurate, and implicit finite-difference scheme. The nonlinear discrete equations were solved by using a nonlinear multigrid method. There is, at most, a first-order time step constraint for stability. We demonstrated numerically the convergence of our scheme and presented simulations of phase separation to show the efficiency and accuracy of the new algorithm.

描述本研究的主要目的和范围 →	We have studied numerically the dynamics of the microphase separation of a water-oil-surfactant system.
描述为达到研究目的所选择的方法 →	We developed an efficient and accurate numerical method for solving the two-dimensional time-dependent Ginzburg-Landau model with two order parameters. The numerical method is based on a conservative, second-order accurate, and implicit finite-difference scheme.
简述研究结果和结论 →	We demonstrated numerically the convergence of our scheme and presented simulations of phase separation to show the efficiency and accuracy of the new algorithm.

以下是撰写摘要时常用的英文表述，用来描述研究的主要目的和范围。

- In this paper, we present a new phase-field model including combined effects of edge diffusion, the Ehrlich-Schowoebel barrier, deposition and desorption to simulate epitaxial growth.
- We present efficient and robust multigrid methods for the solution of large, nonlinear, non-smooth systems as resulting from implicit time discretization of vector-valued Allen-Cahn equations with isotropic interfacial energy and logarithmic

potential.

- We present a numerical model for solving the Cahn-Hilliard equation.
- We present a new phase-field model for three-component immiscible liquid flows with surface tension.
- We present efficient, second-order accurate and adaptive finite-difference methods to solve the regularized, strongly anisotropic Cahn-Hilliard equation in 2D and 3D.
- This paper presents a numerical method for the axially symmetrical problem.
- A computationally efficient numerical scheme is presented for the phase-field model of two-phase systems for anisotropic interfacial energy.
- We present a new phase-field method for modeling surface tension effects on multi-component immiscible fluid flows.
- We consider a second-order conservative nonlinear numerical scheme for the N-component Cahn-Hilliard system modeling the phase separation of a N-component mixture.
- We consider an unconditionally gradient stable scheme for solving the Allen-Cahn equation representing a model for anti-phase domain coarsening in a binary mixture.
- A diffuse-interface model is considered for solving axisymmetric immiscible two-phase flow with surface tension.
- An adaptive finite difference method is developed for a class of fully nonlinear time-dependent thin liquid film equations.
- The method is second-order accurate in both space and time.
- The efficiency of the method is demonstrated by applying it for a variety of selected equations.
- We demonstrate performance of the proposed image segmentation

algorithm on several synthetic and real images to confirm the efficiency and stability of the proposed method.

- The shape of the liquid in this situation has been investigated by both experiment and computer simulation.
- It is shown that both models generate microstructures which are qualitatively similar to those observed experimentally.
- The method suffers from slow convergence when classical iteration methods such as Gauss-Seidel or SOR are employed. In order to alleviate this problem we propose several multigrid techniques that exhibit grid-independent convergence and solve the biharmonic equation in a small amount of computer time.
- A study is made using numerical experiments to see the effect of the parameters in the explicit Euler-discretized form of a one-dimensional, nonlinear, reaction-diffusion equation.

如果论文包含 MATLAB 代码,可以在摘要中使用如下表述。

- The paper is meant to be a practical guide towards solving such problems adaptively and contains an example of a MALTAB code for resolving the singular behaviour of the semi-linear heat equation.
- The complete 88 line code is included as an appendix and can be downloaded from the website www.topopt.dtu.dk.

在描述通过扩展先前研究而获得的研究成果时,可以使用如下表述。

- In this paper we extend our earlier work on the efficient implementation of ENO (essentially non-oscillatory) shock-capturing schemes.
- The simple model developed by Li and Jang for the deformation

of a single ellipsoidal drop in a viscous flow is extended here to predict the drop deformation in confined viscous flows.

- The present study extends the previous two-dimensional research to the three-dimensional space.
- This paper extends results described in ...
- These works are extensions of our earlier work for the one-dimensional case.
- We extend our recent phase-field approach to 3D vesicle dynamics.
- The numerical results are first compared with the predictions of the model by Li and Jang for bulk flow.
- The scheme is simple to implement, can be added to any PIDE solver based on the IMEX Euler scheme, and is remarkably fast and accurate.
- The numerical results are also compared with the theory of Li and Jang which includes the influence of wall effects on deformation.

在摘要中简述研究结果和结论时可参考以下示例。

- Numerical experiments are given to demonstrate the performance of the proposed method.
- Numerical solutions for flows over a backward-facing step are presented and compared with experimental data and other numerical results.
- Numerical experiments indicate that the convergence speed as well is independent of temperature.
- The numerical results show excellent agreement with analytical solutions.
- The results agree well with the linear stability theory.

- We give computational results for the four component fluid flows to illustrate the properties of the method.
- Our simulation results are consistent with previous theories and experimental observations.
- We present numerical experiments demonstrating that our proposed formulation produces co-continuous morphologies in complex domains.
- Numerical simulations confirm the theoretical results.

3.4.2 数值分析类论文摘要

数值分析类的论文一般会提出新的模型和数值技术。读者通常会特别关注论文中新模型的特点和新数值方法的特点。因此以下三点内容需要在摘要中体现。

- Mathematical model (新模型的特点是什么?)
- Numerical method (新的数值方法有什么特点?)
- Numerical tests

如下示例供参考。

- We present efficient and robust multigrid methods for the solution of large, nonlinear, non-smooth systems as resulting from implicit time discretization of vector-valued Allen-Cahn equations with isotropic interfacial energy and logarithmic potential.

摘要中可以使用多种动词时态。

- 使用现在时态

  A numerical method for computing three-dimensional, time-dependent incompressible flows **is** presented. The method **is** based on a fractional-step, or time-splitting, scheme in conjunction with the approximate-factorization technique. It

is shown that the use of velocity boundary conditions for the intermediate velocity field **can** lead to inconsistent numerical solutions. Appropriate boundary conditions for the intermediate velocity field **are** derived and tested. Numerical solutions for flows inside a driven cavity and over a backward-facing step **are** presented and compared with experimental data and other numerical results [11].

• 使用现在时和现在完成时

This paper **considers** the accuracy of projection method approximations to the initialboundary-value problem for the incompressible Navier-Stokes equations. The issue of how to correctly specify numerical boundary conditions for these methods **has been** outstanding since the birth of the second-order methodology a decade and a half ago. It **has been observed** that while the velocity **can** be reliably computed to second-order accuracy in time and space, the pressure is typically only first-order accurate in the L∞norm. This paper **identifies** the source of this problem in the interplay of the global pressure-update formula with the numerical boundary conditions and **presents** an improved projection algorithm which is fully second-order accurate, as demonstrated by a normal mode analysis and numerical experiments. In addition, a numerical method based on a gauge variable formulation of the incompressible Navier-Stokes equations, which **provides** another option for obtaining fully second-order convergence in both velocity and pressure, **is** discussed. The connection between the boundary conditions for projection methods and the gauge method **is** explained in detail [3].

在摘要中，应尽量避免重复，比如不停使用 in this paper，this paper 等。不要使用不熟悉的术语或缩写。应避免使用表格、数字和方程式。尽量不引用表格或图表，也不应引用其他论文。在许多数据库中，读者必须付费才能阅读论文全文，由于参考文献在正文中列出，如果摘要中有参考文献的编号，未付费的读者是无法查看参考文献的。摘要中不得已使用参考文献时，引用的任何信息都必须完整给出。请对比以下摘要示例。

不推荐的摘要示例

We develop a conservative, second-order accurate fully implicit discretization of the Navier-Stokes (NS) and Cahn-Hilliard(CH) system that has an associated discrete energy functional. This system provides a diffuse-interface description of binary fluid flows with compressible or incompressible flow components [3]. In this work, we focus on the case of flows containing two immiscible, incompressible and density-matched components.

推荐的摘要示例

We develop a conservative, second-order accurate fully implicit discretization of the Navier-Stokes (NS) and Cahn-Hilliard(CH) system that has an associated discrete energy functional. This system provides a diffuse-interface description of binary fluid flows with compressible or incompressible flow components [R. Soc. Lond. Proc. Ser. A Math. Phys. Eng. Sci. 454 (1998) 2617]. In this work, we focus on the case of flows containing two immiscible, incompressible and density-matched components.

3.4.3 综述类论文摘要

综述类论文通过系统地总结、分析已有的研究发现，力求为读者呈现某一领域的研究进展。以下是综述类论文摘要示例。

Phase-field models for microstructure evolution [6]

Abstract: The phase-field method has recently emerged as a powerful computational approach to modeling and predicting mesoscale morphological and microstructure evolution in materials. It describes a microstructure using a set of conserved and nonconserved field variables that are continuous across the interfacial regions. The temporal and spatial evolution of the field variables is governed by the Cahn-Hilliard nonlinear diffusion equation and the Allen-Cahn relaxation equation. With the fundamental thermodynamic and kinetic information as the input, the phase-field method is able to predict the evolution of arbitrary morphologies and complex microstructures without explicitly tracking the positions of interfaces. **This paper briefly reviews the recent advances in developing phase-field models for various materials processes including solidification, solid-state structural phase transformations, grain growth and coarsening, domain evolution in thin films, pattern formation on surfaces, dislocation microstructures, crack propagation, and electromigration.**

3.4.4 对比类论文摘要

对比类或比较类论文旨在分析和比较不同研究方法、研究发现等的异同，进而提出自己的观点。以下为对比类论文摘要常用的表述。

- We compare four surface motion laws for sharp surfaces with their diffuse interface counterparts by means of gradient flows on corresponding energy functionals.

可参考以下比较类的摘要示例。

Comparison between advected-field and level set methods in the study of vesicle dynamics [8]

Abstract: Phospholipidic membranes and vesicles constitute a basic element in real biological functions. Vesicles are viewed as a model system to mimic basic viscoelastic behaviors of some cells, like red blood cells. Phase field and level-set models are powerful tools to tackle dynamics of membranes and their coupling to the flow. These two methods are somewhat similar, but to date no bridge between them has been made. This is a first focus of this paper. Furthermore, a constitutive viscoelastic law is derived for the composite fluid: the ambient fluid and the membranes. We present two different approaches to deal with the membrane local incompressibility, and point out differences. Some numerical results following from the level-set approach are presented.

Comparison of finite-volume numerical methods with staggered and collocated grids [15]

Abstract: The paper presents a detailed comparison of two finite-volume solution methods for two-dimensional incompressible fluid flows, one with staggered and the other with colocated numerical grids. The staggered method is well-known and well-established, and it is used here as a standard against which the relatively new colocated approach is compared. Three test cases were considered, employing orthogonal rectilinear grids: lid driven cavity flow, backward facing step flow and flow through a pipe with sudden contraction. The results of the computations demonstrate that the convergence rate, dependency on under-relaxation parameters, computational effort and accuracy are almost identical for both solution methods. The colocated method converges faster in some cases, and has advantages when extensions such as multigrid techniques and non-orthogonal grids are considered.

Comparison of sequence accelerators for the Gaver method of numerical Laplace transform inversion [18]

Abstract: The sequence of Gaver functionals is useful in the numerical inversion of Laplace transforms. The convergence behavior of the sequence is logarithmic, therefore, an acceleration scheme is required. The accepted procedure utilizes Salzer summation, because in many cases the Gaver functionals have the asymptotic behavior $f_n(t) - f_{n-1}(t) \sim An^2$ as $n \to \infty$ for fixed t. It seems that no other acceleration schemes have been investigated in this area. Surely, the popular nonlinear methods should be more effective. However, to our surprise, only one nonlinear method was superior to Salzer summation, namely the Wynn's rho algorithm.

Comparison study for level set and direct Lagrangian methods for computing Willmore flow of closed planar curves [5]

Abstract: The main goal of this paper is to present results of comparison study for the level set and direct Lagrangian methods for computing evolution of the Willmore flow of embedded planar curves. To perform such a study we construct new numerical approximation schemes for both Lagrangian as well as level set methods based on semi-implicit in time and finite/complementary volume in space discretizations. The Lagrangian scheme is stabilized in tangential direction by the asymptotically uniform grid point redistribution. Both methods are experimentally second-order accurate. Moreover, we show precise coincidence of both approaches in case of various elastic curve evolutions provided that solving the linear systems in semiimplicit level set method is done in a precise way, redistancing is performed occasionally and the influence of boundary conditions on the level set function is eliminated.

Phase-field versus level set method for 2D dendritic growth [16]

Abstract: The goal of the paper is to review and compare two of the most popular methods for modeling the dendritic solidification in 2D, that tracks the interface between phases implicitly, e.g. the phase-field method and the level set method. We apply these methods to simulate the dendritic crystallization of a pure melt. Numerical experiments for different anisotropic strengths are presented. The two methods compare favorably and the obtained tip velocities and tip shapes are in good agreement with the microscopic solvability theory.

Comparing numerical methods for response of beams with moving mass [4]

Abstract: In this paper, we applied two methods to solve a class of linear differential equation with initial conditions using Adomian's decomposition and homotopy perturbation methods. We present analytical and numerical methods that can be used to determine the dynamic behavior of beams, with different boundary conditions, carrying a moving mass.

A comparison of numerical models for one-dimensional Stefan problems [9]

Abstract: In this paper, we present a critical comparison of the suitability of several numerical methods, level set, moving grid and phase field model, to address two well-known Stefan problems in phase transformation studies: melting of a pure phase and diffusional solid-state phase transformations in a binary system. Similarity solutions are applied to verify the numerical results. The comparison shows that the type of phase transformation considered determines the convenience of the numerical techniques. Finally, it is shown both numerically and analytically that the solid-solid phase transformation is a limiting case of the solid and liquid transformation.

Mumford-Shah based registration: A comparison of a level set and a phase-field approach [7]

Abstract: Traditionally, different image processing tasks are mainly considered on their own. The main aim of this paper is a combination of registration, i.e., the spatial alignment of images and segmentation, i.e., the recognition of edges and object contours in images. A proper registration depends on a good initial segmentation and vice versa. In this paper, it is proposed to link these problems together by formulating a coupled variational problem. We will focus on an edgebased approach instead of considering image intensities and propose a variational formulation based on the Mumford and Shah free discontinuity problem. This paper is particularly devoted to a comparison of a sharp interface approach with the phase field analogue.

在撰写摘要时，如果从其他论文中借鉴了某些表述，在之后修改时需要转述。在这种情况下，最好用颜色对它们进行标记，这样在后续修改时可以轻松识别并加以修正。

3.4.5 关键词

论文需要列出反映文章主题和核心思想的关键词。读者会通过检索关键词来筛选与个人研究相关的论文。因此，关键词需要谨慎选择和使用。此外，不要在关键字的末尾加上句点。

根据期刊要求的不同，关键词可以用分号或逗号分隔，如下所示。

- Image segmentation; Mumford-Shah functional; Chan-Vese model; Allen-Cahn equation; phase-field method; gradient descent method

- Image segmentation, Mumford-Shah functional, Chan-Vese model, Allen-Cahn equation, phase-field method, gradient descent method

3.5 引言

引言部分主要介绍研究的背景和目的。该部分不仅需要阐述论文的研究问题、研究目的和研究方法,还要说明本研究的科学意义,并简单概述已发表的相关论文的研究成果,必要的话也可以简单总结一下相关论文对本研究主题的贡献。引言也会简要回顾研究所涉方程和模型。引言的篇幅通常占论文总篇幅的10%～20%。

3.5.1 引言的主要内容

引言部分大致包含如下内容。

- 研究课题的重要性。
- 现有研究方法以及其局限性。
- 本研究的结果和意义。
- 全文的结构安排。

具体来说,引言中应阐明:研究主题,包括迄今为止该主题涉及的研究范围和研究类型;研究兴趣和既往研究成果;当前研究和以往研究的关系,应特别强调自己的研究在哪些方面优于以往的研究;研究目的以及所建立的假设,在假设的条件下才能考虑所进行研究的创造性和必要性。在撰写引言时,还应注意以下问题:

- 如使用缩写,在其第一次出现时应对其进行定义。即便是已经在摘要中给出定义的缩写,第一次出现在引言中时,也应进行定义。
- 介绍既往研究时应列出相关方程应用的例子,同时,应引用相关的论文。

3.5.2 引言中的常用表达

下面是一些引言部分常用的英文表述，供大家参考。

- In recent years, nonlinear partial differential equations of Black-Scholes type have attracted the attention of many researchers in the field if computational finance.
- A lot of research work has been done in coupling the FE method with the BE method [1-3] and the finite difference (FD) method with the BE method [2].
- Recently, there has been growing interest in ...
- The impact of a droplet has been studied extensively in the literature from theoretical, computational, and experimental points of view.
- An investigation is made on the effect of the parameters in the explicit Euler-discretized form of a nonlinear reaction-diffusion equation.
- Among the many numerical methods that simulate multiphase fluid flows, the phasefield model has attracted the most popular attention.
- Soluble iron plays a central role in processes.
- Both the solubility and the bioavailability of Fe vary according to differences.
- Unlike batteries, however, fuel cells need to be immersed in a constant supply of fuel.
- However, the technique has limitations.
- Two competing models exist in the literature [1-3].
- The migration rate increases with mass-ratio q and decreases with distance Δ.

- The AC equation and its various modified equations have been applied to a wide range of problems such as phase transitions [1], image analysis (gray and colour image segmentation, image inpainting) [2], the motion by mean curvature [3], two-phase fluid flows such as the retraction, pinch-off of a liquid filament, and the formation of drops [4], and crystal growth [5].
- Practical examples include manufacturing processes such as the production of videotapes, photographic films, and microchips [3].
- Many problems arising in control engineering can be easily solved if the system under consideration is described by a proper model.
- One of the important problems is the design of transmission codes.
- The application of numerical solutions is the only way to resolve this problem.
- A different computational approach which models the mask as a pixelated binary image can be found in Ref. [1].
- This paper is concerned with an improvement in a method that was first introduced by Peskin for the study of flow patterns around heart valves [1 - 3]. This IBM has since been applied to a variety of problems in two and three space dimensions, including blood flow [1], wave propagation [2], and aggregation [3].
- There are few attempts, to our knowledge, to use non-reflecting type boundary conditions for the Navier-Stokes equations.

- Although considerable research has been devoted to ..., rather less attention has been paid to ...
- Little mathematical investigation has been carried out for any of the sharp interface models except motion by mean curvature.
- Most of the existing phase-field simulations employed the explicit forward Euler method in time and finite difference in space.
- Only few researchers have addressed this problem and they have done this using 2D imagery.
- The Allen-Cahn(AC) equation was originally introduced as a phenomenological model for antiphase domain coarsening in a binary alloy [1].
- In this paper, we consider an efficient and accurate finite difference multigrid approximation of the Cahn-Hilliard(CH) equation with a variable mobility.
- Chan and Vese proposed the Chan-Vese model.
- The main challenge is that neither the connection between the data points nor the topology of the final shape is known a priori.
- We will discuss this problem in detail.
- It should be emphasized that while the methods will allow one to take arbitrarily large time steps and not become unstable, the accuracy of the numerical solution will depend on choosing a small enough time step to resolve the dynamics.
- **It should be pointed out that** if the function is independent of t, then the function can be written in the form $f(x,t)=g(x)$.

- **It should be noted that** if the function is independent of t, then the function can be written in the form $f(x,t)=g(x)$.
- **It should be remarked that** if the function is independent of t, then the function can be written in the form $f(x,t)=g(x)$.

描述论文研究目的的常见表达方式如下。

- The main purpose of this paper is to present an efficient diffuse-interface phase-field model for elastically inhomogeneous systems.
- However, none of the diffuse-interface or phase-field approximations model the Ehrlich-Schowoebel barrier. It is the purpose of this paper to introduce a diffuse-interface approximation that reproduces the Ehrlich-Schowoebel barrier.
- The main purpose of this article is to introduce a new surface tension force formulation in diffuse-interface models. The novel feature of this new formulation is that it permits the explicit calculation of pressure field from the governing equations.
- The objective of this paper is to describe the extension of our single grid algorithm for the thin film equations [4] to an adaptive mesh refinement algorithm so that we can simulate realistic physical phenomena.
- The objective of this paper is to propose a hybrid scheme for the multi-component CH equation which is an extension of the previous work [1].
- The aim of the present paper is to give ...
- The main purpose of the present paper is to give ...
- It is the aim of this paper to investigate the role of curvature and viscosity.
- In this paper, ...

- In this study, ...
- In this article, ...
- However, we point out that our results can be extended to the more general case.
- In this paper, we will focus on the isotropic regularization. However, the proposed method can be easily extended to other cases as well.
- The CH equation with a constant mobility has been intensively studied with numerical methods (e.g., [1, 2, 3], and the references therein). However, only a few authors (e.g., [4,5]) studied the CH equation with concentration dependent mobility numerically, although it appeared in the original derivation of the equation, see [6].

如果论文中的研究方法或研究发现是首创,可以参考以下常见表达方式。

- To the authors' knowledge, this is the first time when neural networks are being applied to resource discovery problem.
- To the authors' knowledge, there has been no trial to check the accuracy of the SDS model.
- To the author's knowledge, the present study is the first attempt to use the IBM method.
- To the best of our knowledge ...

引言的最后一句或者最后一段一般会说明论文的整体结构和安排。我们可以参考以下内容并灵活使用。

- The outline of this paper is as follows: in Section 2, we describe the discretisation of the equations by a semi-implicit backward Euler method in time and continuous piecewise linear finite elements in space; Section 3 describes the multigrid algorithm; Sections 4 and 5 discuss some numerical results in both one and two space dimensions and in Sections 6 and 7, we look at how adaptive time-stepping and non-uniform meshes effect the solver.

- This paper is organized as follows: In Section 2, we review the governing equations. In Section 3, we derive numerical solution with a nonlinear multigrid method. In Section 4, we present numerical results. Conclusions are made in Section 5.
- The remaining parts of this paper are organized as follows: In Section 2, we describe a phase-field model for the mixture of three immiscible fluids. In Section 3, we give a numerical solution. Representative numerical experiments for ternary fluid flow are provided in Section 4. In Section 5, conclusions are drawn.
- The contents of this paper are as follows: In Section 2, we briefly review the governing equations. In Section 3, we consider a fully discrete semi-implicit finite-difference scheme and describe a nonlinear multigrid V-cycle algorithm for the TDGL system. Numerical experiments such as a second-order convergence test and tests of the effects of parameters on the phase separation of the system are performed in Section 4. In Section 5, conclusions are given. In addition, we present a future direction for this current algorithm. The future plan is to incorporate hydrodynamic effects.
- The contents of this paper are: In Section 2 we discretize the new surface tension force formulation. In Section 4 we present numerical experiments to validate our new surface tension formulation. The experiments are simulations of 2 dimensional

drop, 3 dimensional drop under shear flow, and axisymmetric thread breakup under capillary force. In Section 5, conclusions are given.

- The paper is organized as follows: In Section 2 we derive the regularized, strongly anisotropic Cahn-Hilliard equation. In Section 3 the fully discrete, nonlinear FAS multigrid scheme for the regularized equation is given and in Section 4 we discuss the corresponding block-structured, adaptive MLAT implementation. In Section 5, numerical results are presented. We give some concluding remarks in Section 6. In the Appendix, we discuss the link between the ill-posedness of the sharp and diffuse interface problems.
- The contents of this paper are as follows: In Section 2, we present the coupled NS and CH equations. In Section 3, we derive the discrete scheme, demonstrate the existence of a discrete energy functional. In Section 4, we present the nonlinear multigrid method for the fully discrete system in the absence of flow. In Section 5, we present the approximate projection method used to solve the discrete generalized NS equations. In Section 6, we perform a local mode analysis for the nonlinear multigrid scheme to analyze the smoothing factor. In Section 7, we present numerical results. In Section 8, we discuss future directions and present a simulation of the break-up of a liquid thread under the Rayleigh instability. In Appendix A, the derivation of the smoothing operator for the nonlinear multigrid scheme is presented. In Appendix B, the classical Crank-Nicolson discretization of the CH equation is presented and discussed.

- The paper is organized in the following manner. The governing equation in cylindrical coordinates is introduced in Section 2. The proposed schemes are numerically tested in Section 3. Finally, conclusions are derived in Section 4.
- The contents of this paper are as follows: In Section 2, the governing equations are presented. In Section 3, we derive the discrete scheme, demonstrate the existence of a discrete energy functional and prove stability and convergence of the algorithm. In Section 4, we present numerical experiments.
- The contents of this paper are: In Section 2, governing equations are given. In Section 3, we describe the numerical solution. In Section 4, we present numerical experiments to validate our new augmented projection scheme. In Section 5, conclusions are given.
- The contents of this paper are as follows: In Section 2, the governing equations are derived. In Section 3, we derive the discrete scheme and numerical solution. We also present the approximate projection method used to solve the discrete generalized NS equations. Numerical experiments are presented at Section 4. In Section 5, conclusions are drawn.
- This paper is organized as follows: In Section II we briefly review the governing equations. In Section III, we derive the numerical solution with a nonlinear multigrid method. In Section IV, we present numerical results. Conclusions are made in Section V.
- The contents of this paper are as follows: In Section 2 we briefly review governing equations for phase separation in a N-component system which takes a concentration dependence

of the mobility. In Section 3 we consider a fully discrete semi-implicit finite difference scheme and describe an efficient and accurate nonlinear multigrid V-cycle algorithm for the N-component CH system. We present numerical experiments such as a second-order convergence test, comparison with a linear stability analysis of the equations, the evolution of triple junctions, and phase separation in a quaternary mixture in Section 4. Finally, in Section 5 we conclude.

- This paper is organized as follows: In Section Ⅱ, we briefly review a derivation of the Cahn-Hilliard equation. This derivation is based on constrained gradient dynamics for a physically motivated functional. In Section Ⅲ, we describe the discrete scheme and its properties, such as mass conservation and total energy, decrease. We present the numerical results in Section Ⅳ. Section Ⅴ contains a discussion.
- This paper is organized as follows: In Section 2, we briefly review a derivation of the AC equation, based on gradient dynamics, with a physically motivated functional. In Section 3, we describe the unconditionally gradient stable discrete scheme and its properties such as the total energy decrease and the boundedness of the numerical solution. We present the numerical results in Section 4. In Section 5, we conclude. Appendix follows with details.
- The contents of this paper are organized as follows: In Section 2, we consider a fully discrete semi-implicit finite difference scheme and obtain sufficient stability estimates. Also, we describe a nonlinear multigrid V-cycle algorithm for the ternary CH system. Numerical experiments such as a

second-order convergence test, comparison with linear stability analysis, different boundary conditions, and effects of a concentration dependent mobility are presented in Section 3. Finally, in Section 4 we conclude.

- The outline of the paper is as follows: In Section 2, we propose a phase-field model for four immiscible fluids. In Section 4, we perform some characteristic numerical experiments for quaternary fluid flows. In Section 5, conclusions are drawn.

3.5.3 引言中的时态

引言中的时态一般应保持一致，但也有例外，比如：主句使用过去时态，从句在表达一般真理时应该使用现在时态。例如：

- They pointed out that the energy functional of the Chan-Vese method has no minimizer.
- However, these sharp interface models suffer from several drawbacks: (i) dynamic interfacial tension relies on an asserted equilibrium equation of state, which is also assumed to be valid beyond the equilibrium state; (ii) for interfacial flows with soluble surfactants, mass transfer between the interface and the bulk fluids requires an external boundary condition, which cannot uniquely arise from the model itself; (iii) model extension for more complicated systems, such as ionic surfactant solutions, is not easy [1]; (iv) numerical stability becomes a problem for the flows with large topological changes, such as droplet breakup and coalescence.
- The differences between the proposed model and most prior models are that (1) the present model allows for combinations of both destinations and purposes, whereas

previous models only allow for one of these factors; (2) the present model is easier to estimate and interpret because it is formulated in terms of a nested logit structure that fits in the random utility framework, which allows for measurement error and unobserved attribute effects; (3) this framework enables us to make more direct utility models of SP-SS shopping behavior; and (4) the random utility framework enables rescaling of the conjoint model estimates to the revealed choice data, which increases the external validity of the model.

These models have been proposed to explain how the MA signals the cortex to position the cleavage furrow. The first model is A. The second model is B. The third model is C.

3.5.4 引言参考示例

下面是一篇论文的引言部分，供大家参考。

Energy Stable Schemes for Cahn-Hilliard Phase-Field Model of Two-Phase Incompressible Flows [17]

强调本研究的重要性 → The phase-field approach for multi-phase incompressible flows have attracted much attention recently (cf. [11, 2, 16, 12, 15, 26] and the references therein).

回顾与本研究相关的近期研究

Since the phase-field (or diffusive interface) model can be considered as an approximation to the sharp interface model, one can use the gradient flow based on either the conserved Cahn-Hilliard dynamics (cf. [5]) or the Allen-Cahn dynamics (cf. [1]) with a non-local Lagrange multiplier, leading to the Cahn-Hilliard phase-field model and Allen-Cahn phase-field model, respectively. Both models, at least in the matched density case, can be derived from an energetic variational approach. Thus, they admit an energy law, making it possible to design numerical schemes which satisfy a corresponding discrete energy law that automatically ensures their numerical stability (cf., for instance, [1, 2, 3]).

现有研究的局限性

However, most of the analysis and simulation of the phase-field model for two-phase flows have been restricted to the matched density case or with a Boussinesq approximation. The main difficulty for two-phase flows with different density is that the standard phase-field model with variable density does not admit an energy law, making it difficult to carry out mathematical and numerical analysis. In a recent work (cf. [1]), the authors proposed a phase-field model with variable density which admits an energy law, and constructed efficient and simple energy stable time discretization schemes for the corresponding Allen-Cahn phase-field model.

本研究克服了以往研究结果的局限性 →

The main objective of this paper is to construct efficient and simple energy stable time discretization schemes for the Cahn-Hilliard phase-field model with matched density and variable density. The main additional theoretical and numerical difficulty associated with the Cahn-Hilliard model, as opposed to the Allen-Cahn model, is that the fourth-order spatial derivatives are involved in the Cahn-Hilliard equation for the phase function. By using a mixed formulation for the fourth-order Cahn-Hilliard phase equation and using the chemical potential to reformulate the surface tension term in the momentum equation, we are able to extend the results presented in [23] for the Allen-Cahn phase-field model to the Cahn-Hilliard phase-field model.

本文的结构和安排 →

The rest of the paper is organized as follows. In the next section, we present the Cahn-Hilliard phase-field model for two-phase incompressible flows with matched density and variable density. Then, in Section 3, we construct several efficient time discretization schemes for both matched density and variable density cases, and show that they are unconditionally energy stable. Some numerical results and discussions are presented in the last section.

3.6 研究思想和方法

研究思想和方法部分是论文的核心，它是对所进行研究的评估以及研究设计和研究步骤的详细描述，通过阅读这部分，其他研究人员能够了解研究细节，复制研究。虽然阐述所有技术细节是不现实的，但这部分内容要做到足够详细，以便其他研究人员可以重现本研究。如果论文是在已发表的方法基础上进行改进，需要引述该方法，并描述自己研究中所作出的改进。因为每个期刊要求不同，在撰写这部分之前，请查阅您计划投稿的期刊的格式要求。

3.6.1 控制方程的常用表述

下面给出一些数学领域控制方程的写作示例，供大家参考。

We consider an unconditionally gradient stable algorithm for the AC equation:

$$\frac{\partial c(\mathbf{x}, t)}{\partial t} = -M(F'(c(\mathbf{x},t)) - \epsilon^2 \Delta c(\mathbf{x},t)),\ \mathbf{x} \in \Omega, 0 \leqslant t \leqslant T$$

where $\Omega \subset \mathbf{R}^d (d=1,2,3)$ is a domain. The quantity $c(\mathbf{x}, t)$ is defined to be the difference between the concentrations of the two mixtures' components. The coefficient M is a constant mobility. We take $M \equiv 1$ for convenience. The function $F(c)$ is the Helmholtz free-energy density for c. It has a double well form, i.e., $F(c) = 0.25(c^2 - 1)^2$ as in Ref. [1]. Figure 3-2 shows the function $F(c)$. The small constant ϵ is the gradient energy coefficient related to the interfacial energy. The boundary condition is

$$\frac{\partial c}{\partial \mathbf{n}} = 0 \ on\ \partial\Omega,$$

where $\frac{\partial}{\partial \mathbf{n}}$ denotes the normal derivative on $\partial \Omega$. The physical meaning of the condition is that the total free energy of the mixture decreases in time.

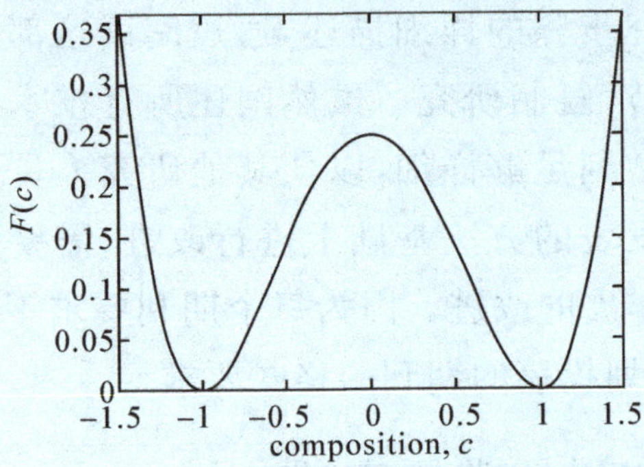

Figure 3-2　A double well potential, $F(c)=0.25(c^2-1)^2$.

The primitive variable formulation of the incompressible Navier-Stokes equations (NSE) on a domain $\Omega \subset \mathbf{R}^2$ (or $\mathbf{R}^3$) takes the form

$$\mathbf{u}_t + (\mathbf{u} \cdot \nabla)\mathbf{u} = -\nabla p + v\,\Delta \mathbf{u},$$
$$\nabla \mathbf{u} = 0,$$

where $\mathbf{u}=(u, v)^T$ (or $\mathbf{u}=(u, v, w)^T$), p, and v are the velocity field, pressure, and kinematic viscosity, respectively. For now we consider the simplest physical boundary condition for $\mathbf{u}$, the no-penetration, no-slip condition

$$\mathbf{u}\,|_{\Gamma} = 0$$

where $\Gamma = \partial\Omega$.

The problem of phase separation in binary mixtures has attracted much interest in recent years. In this paper we shall present and analyse a new model based on the following nonlocal reaction-diffusion equation for $u: \Omega \rightarrow R^1$;

$$u_t = \Delta u - f(u) + \frac{1}{|\Omega|}\int_\Omega f(u)dx \ for\ x \in \Omega,\ t > 0$$

with no-flux boundary conditions

$$\mathbf{n} \cdot \nabla u = 0 \ for\ x \in \partial\Omega$$

and initial data

$$u(x, 0) = g(x).$$

Here, $\Omega \rightarrow R^n$ is a smooth bounded domain with outer unit normal **n** and total volume $|\Omega|$, $f(u) = W'(u)$ where W is the double-well potential depicted in Fig. 1, and g, for simplicity, is taken to be a function satisfying the compatibility condition $\mathbf{n} \cdot \nabla g$ on $\partial\Omega$.

以下是阐述控制方程时有用的表达方式。

- For more details on the derivation and implementation of the optimality criteria method, the reader is referred to the literature [1].
- We refer the reader to [1, 2] for details concerning the equation and physical background of it.
- For additional details about the adaptive multigrid cycle, one may refer to [1].
- The fact that the difference scheme is stable implies that for any j, $\|Q_j\| \leqslant \kappa e^{\beta t}$.
- $F_y + F_{y'} + \cdots = 0$, where the subscripts denote partial derivatives with respect to the corresponding arguments, and

the dots denote terms of order higher than 1 relative to h and h'.

- Periodic boundary conditions are applied along both Cartesian axes.
- When $\delta=0$, Eq. (1) becomes the usual Cahn-Hilliard equation.
- The subscript s in Eq. (1) denotes the partial derivative with respect to s.
- Here t denotes the time variable.
- Suppose $u(x,t)$ satisfies the following first-order linear partial differential equation:

$$a(x,t)\frac{\partial u}{\partial x}-b(x,t)\frac{\partial u}{\partial t}+c(x,t)u=0,$$

where $-\infty<x<+\infty, 0<t<\infty$.

- In the following, the symbol ($*$) is suppressed for the dimensionless variables.
- $\Omega\subset R^d$
- Let the vector field by denoted by x and let ϕ be a weighting factor that is continuously differentiable.
- $\frac{\partial\varphi}{\partial y}$, where the derivatives of φ are evaluated at (x,t).
- The new variables are chosen to be

$$x_t=\frac{N_t}{k}, y_t=\frac{eP_t}{hk}, \text{ and } c=bk.$$

- $\frac{\partial u}{\partial t}=\frac{\partial^2 u}{\partial x^2}$, where u denotes a concentration, x a spatial coordinate, and t time.
- In this section, we shall first review the two-order parameter model proposed by Laradji et al.
- The term $rN_t(1-N_t/K)$ represents logistic growth.
- A change of variable reduces the model to a simpler form.

- It minimizes the sum of the squared error between the output value of network and the real target value.
- P and Q denote predator and prey densities, respectively.
- Note that our method dose not split the energy for Eq. (1) into convex and concave parts.
- An overview of the CH equation will be given in this section in order for the readers to understand the phase-field modeling.
- From now on we use boldface characters for vectors.
- With the unknown curve C, the level-set function $\varphi(x)$ is defined as, ...
- In other words, we define the function as $\varphi(x)=\pm d$, where d is the distance from x to C and the plus(minus) sign is chosen if the point x is outside (inside) C.
- In all these studies, the Cahn-Hilliard equation is endowed with Neumann or periodic boundary conditions.
- $y' = y(1-y)$, where we have omitted the independent variable t on which each function depends.
- The construction of such φ will be given later.
- Our model is formulated in terms of predator and prey densities, $P(x, t)$ and $Q(x, t)$, where x denotes position in the one- or two-dimensional domain and t is time.
- Scaffold is degraded by diffusion, by advection, and so on.
- A PDE model is developed for modeling a bio phenomenon.
- In this paper, we do not go any further into the study of shocks. Instead we refer the interested reader to the survey article by P.D. Lax.

3.6.2 数值方法的常用表述

研究思想和方法部分会对研究方法进行详细阐述，以便具有相关基础知识的研究人员可以复制研究，实现研究结果。必要的话，可以适当使用表格和图片来展示研究结果。这部分的内容应尽可能详细，方便读者理解。

下面首先列出了一些常见表述，用来解释论文中常用的符号。

- Express the roots in terms of the coefficients.
- The solution is determined uniquely up to an additive constant.
- ϕ^3, where the superscript 3 is an exponent.
- $v^n = g^n$. Note that the superscript on v is an index of the time level, while on g it is a power.
- Numerical solution is described in Appendix A.
- The present work focuses on the 2D case but can be straightforwardly extended to 3D.
- For simplicity but without loss of generality, we restrict our analysis to two dimensions (2D).
- For simplicity, we consider only the two-dimensional case.
- In this section, we present fully discrete schemes for the CH equation. In addition, we prove discrete versions of mass conservation and energy dissipation, which immediately imply the stability of the numerical scheme. We shall first discretize the CH equation (1) and (2) in two dimensional space, i.e., $\Omega=(a,b)\times(c,d)$. One- and three-dimensional discretizations are analogously defined. Let N_x and N_y be positive even integers, $h=(b-a)/N_x$ be the uniform mesh size, and $\Omega_h=\{(x_i, y_j): x_i=(i-0.5)h, y_j=(j-0.5)h, 1\leqslant i\leqslant N_x, 1\leqslant j\leqslant N_y\}$ be the set of cell-centers.
- The Fourier transform of the characteristic function is performed analytically and numerically in one-, two-, and three-dimensional spaces.
- The BS equation is discretized on a non-uniform grid defined

by $x_0=0$ and $x_{i+1}=x_i+h_i$ for $i=0, \cdots, N_x-1$, where N_x is the total number of grid points and h_i is the grid spacing, see Fig. 3-3.

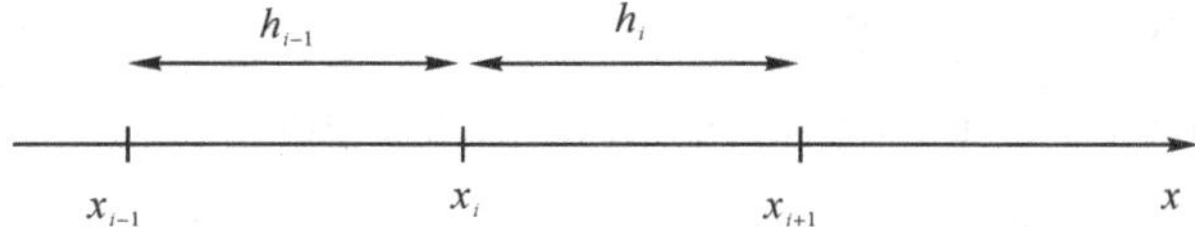

Fig. 3-3 A non-uniform grid with N_x points and grid spacing h_i.

Let c_{ij} and μ_{ij} be approximations of $c(x_i, y_j)$ and $\mu(x_i, y_j)$. We first implement the zero Neumann boundary condition(3) by requiring that

$$D_x c_{i+\frac{1}{2}, j} = D_x c_{N_x+\frac{1}{2}, j} = D_y c_{i, j+\frac{1}{2}} = D_y c_{i, N_y+\frac{1}{2}} = 0,$$

where the discrete differentiation operators are

$$D_x c_{i+\frac{1}{2}, j} = \frac{c_{i+1, j} - c_{ij}}{h}, \quad D_y c_{i, j+\frac{1}{2}} = \frac{c_{i, j+1} - c_{ij}}{h}$$

And we use the notation $\nabla_d c_{ij} = (D_x c_{i+\frac{1}{2}, j}, D_y c_{i, j+\frac{1}{2}})$ to represent the discrete gradient of c at cell-edges. Correspondingly, the divergence at cell-centers, using values from cell-edges, is $\nabla_d \cdot (g^1, g^2)_{ij} = (g^1_{i+\frac{1}{2}, j} - g^1_{i-\frac{1}{2}, j} + g^2_{i, j+\frac{1}{2}} - g^2_{i, j-\frac{1}{2}})/h$. We then define the discrete Laplacian by $\Delta_d c_{ij} = \nabla_d \cdot \nabla_d c_{ij}$ and the discrete l_2 inner product by

$$(c, d)_h = h^2 \sum_{i=1}^{N_x} \sum_{j=1}^{N_y} c_{ij} d_{ij}$$

$$(\nabla_d c, \nabla_d d)_e = h^2 \left(\sum_{i=0}^{N_x} \sum_{j=1}^{N_y} D_x c_{i+\frac{1}{2}, j} D_x d_{i+\frac{1}{2}, j} + \sum_{i=0}^{N_x} \sum_{j=1}^{N_y} D_y c_{i, j+\frac{1}{2}} D_y d_{i, j+\frac{1}{2}} \right)$$

We also define discrete norms as $\|c\|^2 = (c, c)_h$ and $|c|_1^2 = (\nabla_d c, \nabla_d d)_e$.

- $\boldsymbol{n} \cdot \nabla \phi = \boldsymbol{n} \cdot \nabla \mu = 0$, where $\boldsymbol{n}$ is the unit vector normal to $\partial \Omega$.
- Straightforward explicit time-marching requires that time steps be very small in order to maintain numerical stability.

如果基本思想相同，则可以使用 For simplicity of exposition 等表述方式，同时将空间简单地描述为一维，因为在二维或三维中描述时表述会变得比较复杂。以下是一些示例。

- For the sake of simplicity, we assume that the mesh spacings in the x- and y-directions are equal.
- For simplicity, we discretize both space and time with uniform mesh spacings of Δx and t, respectively.
- In this section, we propose an unconditionally stable second-order hybrid numerical method for the Allen-Cahn equation. **For simplicity of exposition**, we shall discretize the AC equation in one-dimensional space, i. e., $\Omega=(a, b)$. Two- and three-dimensional discretizations are defined analogously. JP Let N be a positive even integer, $h=(b-a)/N$ be the uniform grid size, and $\Omega_h=\{x_i=(i-0.5)h, 1\leqslant i\leqslant N\}$ be the set of cell-centers. Let c_i^n be approximations of $c(x_i, n\Delta t)$, where $\Delta t=T/N_t$ is the time step, T is the final time, and N_t is the total number of time steps. We first implement the zero Neumann boundary condition, Eq. (1), by requiring that for each n,
$$\nabla_h c_{\frac{1}{2}}^n = \nabla_h c_{N+\frac{1}{2}}^n = 0 \tag{1}$$
where the discrete differentiation operator is $\nabla_h c_{i+\frac{1}{2}}^n=(c_{i+1}^n - c_i^n)/h$.
- Now we present fully discrete schemes for the Eqs. (4) and (5) in two dimensional space, i. e., $\Omega=(a,b)\times(c,d)$. Let N_x and N_y be positive even integers, $\Delta x=(b-a)/N_x$ be the uniform mesh size, and $\Omega_{\Delta x}=\{(x_i, y_j): x_i=(i-0.5)\Delta x, y_j=(j-0.5)\Delta y, 1\leqslant i\leqslant N_x, 1\leqslant j\leqslant N_y\}$ be the set of cell-centers.

此外，还需要对论文使用的方案(scheme)进行说明，并通过离散化(discretization)方法描述数值解法的性质(property)。这部分内容可以分成小节(subsection)单独叙述。下面是一些常用表述，供大家参考。

- The term ϵ is a computational constant employed to avoid division by zero.
- We propose the following operator splitting scheme, which is unconditionally stable second-order accurate hybrid scheme.

$$\frac{c_i^* - c_i^n}{\Delta t} = \frac{1}{2}(\Delta_h c_i^* + \Delta_h c_i^n),$$

$$\frac{c_i^{n+1} - c_i^*}{\Delta t} = \frac{c_i^{n+1} - (c_i^{n+1})^3}{\epsilon^2}$$

We can consider Eq. (3 - 12) as a Crank-Nicolson scheme for $c_t = \Delta c$ with an initial condition c^n.

- We present a semi-implicit time (Crank-Nicolson) and centered difference space discretization of Eqs. (4) and (5).
- The term ϵ is a computational constant employed to avoid division by zero.
- We use $\Delta t_{\min}$ and $\Delta t_{\max}$ are used to avoid using too small and too large time steps, respectively.
- We repeat the proof for the sake of completeness.
- For the sake of completeness, we give the proofs in the Appendix.
- Having determined these parameters we obtain an analytic solution $u(x, t)$ in a closed form.
- The resulting system of equations is solved by a nonlinear multigrid method.
- A detailed description of the adaptive data structure can be found in [1].
- An interested reader can find details of the numerical algorithm in [1, 2].
- We summarize the above results as follows.
- The points c_k ($k = 0, 1, 2$) lie in the interior of the circular region.
- The quantities Δu_{ij}^n and Δw_{ij}^n are computed in a similar

manner.

- We can rewrite Eq. (1) as
$$u_t + a(x)u_x = -a'(x)u.$$
- Substituting Eq.(2) into Eq. (1) results in $E=mc^2$.
- Substitution of Eqs.(1) and (2) into Eq. (3) gives
$$E = mc^2.$$
- In what follows, the method will be reviewed briefly because details can be found in [1 - 3].
- The proofs will all be based on the following remark: If $\leqslant x_n \leqslant s_n$ for $n \geqslant N$, where N is some fixed numbered, and if $s_n \to 0$, $x_n \to 0$.
- Brief details of the derivation of Eq. (1) are given in the Appendix.
- Detailed information can be found in [1].
- The detailed descriptions can be found in [1 - 3].
- Details of the algorithms employed herein can be found in references [1].
- The staggered grids of Harlow and Welch [1] are used for velocity and pressure fields. However, this type of boundary conditions requires a large distance x. This leads to heavy CPU time and memory storage.
- This is calculated by the Poisson equation $\Delta\phi = f$.

3.7 数值结果

对数值结果的阐述应该简洁明了。数值结果部分一般以一个总结性的句子开头，该句子要能够简明扼要地概况数值实验的主要内容。具体示例如下。

- To demonstrate the capability of our reconstructing scheme, several sets of synthetic and real medical data are used in the experiments.

- In order to demonstrate the efficiency and accuracy of the proposed method, we consider the following examples.
- We start with an example which illustrates the basic mechanism of the algorithm.
- We start with the study of the CH equation in 1D because it is faster then 2D and 3D and there are many results which can be used to compare with our simulations.
- In this section we give the results of numerical calculations upon our model.
- In this section we investigate the performance of our spatial and temporal discretization strategies for the general Cahn-Hilliard model.

以下是针对具体条件的表述方式举例。

描述初始条件

- The initial state is a random perturbation of maximum amplitude 0.05 around $\phi=0$.
- The initial condition is

$$h(x, y, 0) = 0.5\{h_\infty + b - (h_\infty - b)tanh[3(y-7) + rand(x, y)]\}$$

  on a domain $\Omega=(0,200)\times(0,400)$.
- The initial condition is as follows: ...
- We set the initial condition to be $\phi^0=0.0+\eta$, where η is a small random perturbation across the surface.
- We take the initial condition as follows: ...
- The SOR iteration is stopped when the maximum difference of consecutive iterates becomes smaller than a tolerance $\varepsilon=10^{-6}$: $\|u^{n,k}-u^{n,k-1}\|_\infty<\varepsilon$.

- The initial condition is small random perturbation of the stationary solution u^* and v^*.
- The initial condition is the same as in Eq. (1).
- The initial condition is the same as that in Fig. 1.

描述边界条件

- To avoid boundary effects in the simulations we have chosen periodic boundary conditions.

描述空间步长和时间步长

- N_x and N_y are the number of cells in the x- and y- directions, respectively.
- 128×256 grid points, time step $\Delta t=1.0$, and $\epsilon^3=100$ are used.
- The time step is chosen as $\Delta t=0.1h$, where h is the mesh size.
- The time step is 0.01 and the mesh size is 0.0390625.
- The computation is done on a 256×256 grid.
- Numerical solutions of Eqs. (1) and (2) are obtained on a rectangular domain of dimensions $[0,1]$ in x and $[0,2]$ in y using a uniform mesh of 64×128 grid points.
- Numerical solutions are obtained on a domain $\Omega=(0,1)\times(0,1)$ using a mesh of 128×128 grid points.
- We used a domain of size 2×1.
- We tested our method with grid resolutions of 32×32, 64×64, and 128×128.
- The results using the PROST method for three different grid levels (32×32, 64×64, and 128×128) are compared with the analytical solution in Fig. 1.
- The effective fine resolution is 1024×2048.

- The present computations are carried out with $64\times128\times256$ grid points.
- The time-step Δt in the numerical simulations equals 0.001.
- The time step chosen was $\Delta t=0.1h$.
- In all computations, we have fixed the physical parameters to be $\rho=1, \eta=0.01, \sigma=0.1$, and the computational parameters to be $h=0.1$ and $\Delta t=0.01$.
- The parameters used are $Re=100$, $We=1$, and $Pe=100$.
- The parameter values are $a=2$ and $b=3$.
- The parameters we have used are $Re=100$ and $Pe=20$.
- The computational parameters are the same as in Refs. [1,2,3].
- The computational parameters are the same as the above case except the Mach number (M) is set to 0.2.

为了体现通过数值模拟获得的数值结果的可靠性和有效性，论文中需要给出所使用计算机或执行程序所涉及的参数。常见表述如下。

- The algorithms are implemented in MATLAB and carried out on a desktop computer of Intel Xeon CPU E5-1620 3.60GHz processor.
- All the algorithms are implemented using MATLAB for testing purposes, and the computations are carried out on an IBM RS/6000 43P Model 260 workstation.
- Tests were performed on a 3 GHz Intel Pentium with 3 GB of RAM loaded with MATLAB 2009 [1].
- The proposed model was implemented by MATLAB 7 on a computer with Intel Core 2 Duo 2.2 GHz CPU, 2G RAM, and Windows XP operating system.
- We performed our computations in MATLAB 7 software on a

Pentium IV, 2800 MHz CPU machine with 1 GB of memory.

- All coding is done in MATLAB.
- The programs are executed on a standard Pentium D, 3 Ghz desktop PC.
- All computations are performed in MATLAB R2010b environment on a dual 3.10 GHz and 4 GB Intel PC.

结果部分参数的详细程度对结果的复现有很大的影响,可参考以下表述方式对参数进行说明。

- We give an example to test our code(the example is taken from Ref. [1]).
- For expositional simplicity, we focus on the standard lognormal Black-Scholes setting.
- Solutions are computed up to time $t=0.5$.
- We have performed simulations for $h=0.001$ and verified that the results are not much different from the case of $h=1$.
- A=B=C=0, where in the last equality we used the fact that ϕ satisfies Eq.(1).
- We have shown that ϕ also satisfies Eq.(1).
- Therefore, the integral curves of **V** in **Ω** are given by

$$x^2+y^2=c_1,\ z=c_2.$$

- Equations (3 – 14) describe circles parallel to the(x, y)-plane and centered on the z-axis (see Fig. 1).
- Since our PDE based algorithms are iterative procedures, different convergence criterion will give different convergence times.

收敛测试(Convergence test)案例

The method of manufactured exact solutions [10]

We consider one-dimensional Landau-Lifshitz equation with a source:

$$\mathbf{m}_t = -\mathbf{m} \times \mathbf{m}_{xx} + \mathbf{f} \text{ on } \Omega = (0,1)$$

An exact solution of Eq. (3 - 15) is

$$\mathbf{m}^e = \begin{pmatrix} u^e \\ v^e \\ w^e \end{pmatrix} = \begin{pmatrix} \cos(x^2(1-x)^2)\sin(t) \\ \sin(x^2(1-x)^2)\sin(t) \\ \cos(t) \end{pmatrix}.$$

In its component form, the forcing term $\mathbf{f} = \mathbf{m}_t^e + \mathbf{m}^e \times \mathbf{m}_{xx}^e$ can be calculated as follows:

$$\mathbf{f} = \begin{pmatrix} \cos(X)\cos(t) + [(X')^2\sin(X) - X''\cos(X)]\sin(t)\cos(t) \\ \sin(X)\cos(t) - [(X')^2\cos(X) - X''\sin(X)]\sin(t)\cos(t) \\ -\sin(t) + X''\sin^2(t) \end{pmatrix},$$

where $X = x^2(1-x)^2$. Now, we will solve Eq. (3 - 15) with an initial condition $\boldsymbol{m}(x, 0) = (0, 0, 1)$ and zero Neumann boundary condition; i.e., $\boldsymbol{m}_x = 0$ at $\partial\Omega = \{0, 1\}$. We define the numerical error $\boldsymbol{e}_i^n = \boldsymbol{m}_i^n - \boldsymbol{m}^e(x_i, t^n)$ for $i = 1, 2, \cdots, N_x$. The discrete l_2-norm and the maximum norm are defined as

$$\|e^n\|_{l_2} = \sqrt{\sum_{1\leqslant i\leqslant N_x} \frac{\boldsymbol{e}_i^n \cdot \boldsymbol{e}_i^n}{3N_x}} \text{ and } \|e^n\|_\infty = \max_{1\leqslant i\leqslant N_x}\sqrt{\boldsymbol{e}_i^n \cdot \boldsymbol{e}_i^n}.$$

To obtain an estimate of the convergence rate, we performed a number of simulations on a set of increasingly finer grids. We computed the numerical solutions on uniform grids, $h = 1/2^n$ for $n = 6, 7, 8, 9$, and 10. For each case, we ran the calculation to time $T = 1$ with a time step $\Delta t = 0.32h$. The errors and rates of convergence are given in Table 3 - 1. The results suggest that the scheme is indeed second-order accurate in space and time.

Table 3 - 1 The l_2 and maximum norms and convergence rates with space step $h=1/N_x$, time step $\Delta t=0.32h$, total time $T=1$, and an iteration convergence tolerance of 10^{-10}.

Case	64	Rate	128	Rate	256	Rate	512	Rate	1024
$\|e^n\|_{l_2}$	6.5E-5	1.99	1.6E-5	1.99	4.1E-6	2.00	1.0E-6	2.00	2.5E-7
$\|e^n\|_\infty$	1.1E-4	1.99	2.7E-5	1.99	6.7E-6	2.00	1.7E-6	1.99	4.2E-7

存在真实解的测试案例

To obtain an estimate of the rate of convergence, we performed a number of simulations for a sample initial problem on a set of increasingly finer grids. We considered a domain, $\Omega=[0,300]\times[0,300]$. We computed the numerical solutions on uniform grids, $h=300/2^n$ for $n=5,6,7$, and 8. For each case, we ran the calculation to time $T=0.1$ with a uniform time step depending on a mesh size, $\Delta t=0.032/2^n$. The initial condition is Eq. (1) with $K=1$ and $X_1=X_2=100$. The volatilities are $\sigma_1=0.5$ and $\sigma_2=0.5$. The correlation is $\rho=0.5$, and the riskless interest rate is $r=0.03$. We let e be the error matrix with components $e_{ij}=u(x_i,\ y_j)-u_{ij}$. $u(x_i,\ y_j)$ is the analytic solution of Eq. (2) and u_{ij} is the numerical solution. We compute its discrete L^2 norm $\|e\|_2$ is defined

$$\|e\|_2=\sqrt{\frac{1}{N_xN_y}\sum_{i=1}^{N_x}\sum_{j=1}^{N_y}e_{ij}^2}.$$

The errors and rates of convergence are given in Table 3 - 2. The results show that the scheme is first-order accurate.

Table 3 - 2　The L^2 norms of errors and convergence rates for u at time $T=0.1$.

Case	32×32	Rate	64×64	Rate	128×128	Rate	256×256
$\|e\|_2$	0.028161	0.95	0.014562	1.07	0.006928	0.96	0.003572

不存在真实解的测试案例

To obtain an estimate of the rate of convergence, we perform a number of simulations for a sample initial problem on a set of increasingly finer grids. The initial state for this convergence test on a domain, $\Omega=(0,1)\times(0,1)$, is

$$c^0(x,y)=0.5+0.17\cos(\pi x)\cos(2\pi y)+0.2\cos(3\pi x)\cos(\pi y)$$

The numerical solutions are computed on the uniform grids, $h=1/2^n$ for $n=5,6,7,8$, and 9. For each case, the calculation is run to time $T=0.3$ with the uniform time step, $\Delta t=0.1h$, and $\epsilon=0.01$.

We define the error of a grid to be the discrete l_2-norm of the difference between that grid and the average of the next finer grid cells covering it:

$$e_{h/\frac{h}{2}ij} = c_{hij} - (c_{\frac{h}{2}2i,\,2j} + c_{\frac{h}{2}2i-1,\,2j} c_{\frac{h}{2}2i,\,2j-1} + c_{\frac{h}{2}2i-1,\,2j-1})/4$$

The rate of convergence is defined as the ratio of successive errors: $\log_2 \dfrac{\| e_{h/\frac{h}{2}} \|}{\| e_{\frac{h}{2}/\frac{h}{4}} \|}$.

The errors and rates of convergence are given in Table 3 - 3. The results suggest that the scheme is indeed second order accurate in space and time.

Table 3 - 3　Convergence results—Concentration c.

Case	32—64	Rate	64—128	Rate	128—256	Rate	256—512
l_2	2.90e-02	2.37	5.61e-03	2.03	1.38e-03	2.01	3.43e-04

3.8 表格和图片

如果期刊的作者指南中没有要求必须将图片放在稿件的末尾，那么请将其放在正文中间，这样做可以节省审稿人的工作量。

3.8.1 表格和图片的标题

本小节介绍表格和图片标题的书写。一般表格的标题位于表格的上方，图片的标题位于图片的下方。文字环绕表格或图形的情况是不允许的。

表格或图片的标题没必要用一个完整的句子，但应包含必要的所有信息，以便使读者更好地理解表格或图片的内容。以下是一些表格或图片的标题示例。

- Overlayed original and optimized masks
- Comparison of theoretical results with experiment for Marangoni-stress-driven flows on a vertical plate
- Solutions obtained from the closed-form formulae of the Black-Scholes equation for European option with varying time to maturity
- The graphs of the free energies. Solid curve: equation (1); dotted curve: equation (2).
- Schematic illustration of the two immiscible fluids and surfactant system
- Schematic of a compound liquid jet
- Flow schematic for a capsule deforming in shear flow
- Optimal length L^* against α with varying ϵ
- Time history of drag coefficient for flow over a transversely oscillating circular cylinder at $Re=100$: (a) $\alpha=1, \beta=1$; (b)

$\alpha=2, \beta=2$; and (c) $\alpha=3, \beta=3$.

3.8.2 正文中对表格和图片的描述

表格主要用于表示数值方法的收敛程度。常见表达方述如下。

- Table 1 demonstrates the second-order accuracy of our approach as we refine the grid.
- Table 1 shows the convergence rate of the scheme.

在解释文中的表格和图片时，如果图片或者表格的名字位于句首，一般不缩写，但也有一些期刊要求缩写。图片或者表格的名字在其他位置时，一般使用缩写。

- Figure 1 shows the evolution of spinodal decomposition.
- Figures 3(a) and(b) show . . . .
- These are shown schematically in Fig. 3.
- The top row of this figure shows a conventional GAC leaking through this boundary, while the bottom row shows a region-based GAC implemented using (1).
- As can be seen from Fig. 1, the wavelength is not constant along the axis.
- As can be seen in Fig. 1, there is a truly pronounced difference between the curves.
- As we can see from Fig. 1, the wavelength is not constant along the axis.
- As we can see in Fig. 1, there is a truly pronounced difference between the curves.
- The velocities are interpolated using all the Eulerian values around point $\mathbf{x}$, as illustrated in Fig. 1.
- This solution is shown by the heavy curve in Fig. 2.

- This solution is graphed in Fig. 1.
- Note also that the following figures show only the part of the computational domain between $x=5$ and $x=20$, since this contains all the essential features.
- Figure 1.5.1 shows a sequence of evolving profiles during relaxation. Profiles are shown at equal time intervals after every 25 time steps.
- The evolution of spinodal decomposition is shown in Fig. 1.
- Figures 1(a) and 1(b) follow the evolution of the fluid front as a function of time.
- Figure 1 shows a comparison between computed results and the Marangoni-stress-driven experiments of Cazabat et al. [1].
- The simulation is shown enlarged in Fig. 3.7.
- The entire process is illustrated schematically in Fig. 1.
- The simulation domain is schematically illustrated in Fig. 1.
- In Fig. 2, we plot the solutions at $t=0, 0.1, 0.2, 0.5$.
- Figure 2 shows the evolution of the fluid front at $t=0, 1875$, and 2850.
- Figure 1 shows L^* as a function of α.
- Figures 5(a)–(d) are the computational results.

3.8.3 图片的注意事项

创建图片时，要注意图片中字体的大小和相关文字的表述方式，以便读者能够快速准确地理解图片内容。数字刻度的字号大小大约是文本字号大小的80%。此外，记得把图片打印出来，检查要显示的内容是否清晰可见。

3.8.4 图片版权的获得方式

如果您需要使用以前发表的论文(包括您自己发表的论文)中的图片,必须获得出版商的许可,并在图片的标题中进行说明。比如:

- Reprinted from Bearer et al. [3], with permission from the American Association for Cancer Research.
- Reprinted with permission from Liu et al. [1]. Copyright 2009 by the American Physical Society.
- Reprinted from Carlson et al. [1] with permission from Elsevier Science.
- With kind permission from Springer Science + Business Media, Journal of Mathematical Biology, Nonlinear simulation of solid tumor growth using a mixture model: invasion and branching, Vol. 58, 2009, p. 723, V. Cristini, X. Li, J.S. Lowengrub and S.M. Wise.

获得出版商版权许可的操作步骤请参考下列图示(图 3-1 至图 3-3)。

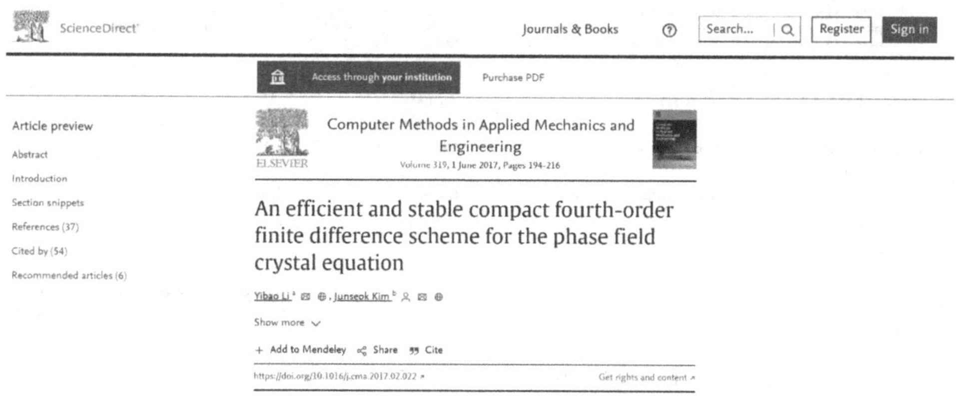

图 3-1 寻找论文所在期刊的版权许可链接

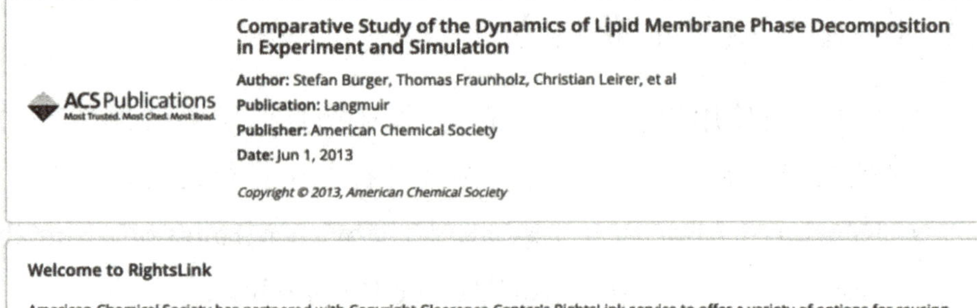

图 3－2　选择“reuse in a journal”

This service provides permission for reuse only. If you do not have a copy of the portion you are using, you may copy and paste the content and reuse according to the terms of your agreement. Please be advised that obtaining the content you license is a separate transaction not involving RightsLink.

If credit is given to another source for the material you requested from RightsLink, permission must be obtained from that source.

Note: Individual Scheme and Structure reuse is free of charge and does not require a license. If the scheme or structure is identified as a Figure in the article, permission is required.

Permission for this particular request is granted for print and electronic formats, and translations, at no charge. Figures and tables may be modified. Appropriate credit should be given. Please print this page for your records and provide a copy to your publisher. Requests for up to 4 figures require only this record. Five or more figures will generate a printout of additional terms and conditions. Appropriate credit should read: "Reprinted with permission from {COMPLETE REFERENCE CITATION}. Copyright {YEAR} American Chemical Society." Insert appropriate information in place of the capitalized words.

I would like to...	reuse in a Journal	Format	Electronic
Requestor Type	Author (original work)	Select your currency	USD - $
Portion	Table/Figure/Micrograph	Quick Price	Click Quick Price
Number of Table/Figure/Micrographs	1		

QUICK PRICE　CONTINUE

图 3－3　填写相关信息，获取图片版权

3.9 结论

一般来说，大多数读者在阅读论文时会首先阅读摘要和结论两个部分，因此结论部分的撰写也是十分重要的。结论部分要对主要研究成果进行系统且清晰的总结，不仅需要说明研究成果的可应用性，而且应指出未来的研究方向。结论部分可以以摘要作为参考，但是内容还是要重新撰写的。一般来说，结论部分大约三分之一的篇幅概述摘要的内容，三分之一描述研究中有意义的结果和发现，剩下的三分之一展望未来研究的主题。以下是可以用来描述未来研究方向的英文表述示例。

- **In future work**, we will investigate the effects of edge diffusion, anisotropy and elastic interactions as these phenomena can play a critical role in step meandering and bunching instabilities.
- **As future research** the methodology introduced in this paper can be combined with a fast summation technique.
- More extensive three-dimensional simulations and more detailed analysis will be carried out **in our future works**.
- Work on the global stability analysis of the scheme (1) is under investigation and will be submitted soon.

撰写研究论文的结论时，切忌不加任何考虑就使用过去时。在描述一般事实时应使用现在时。具体例子如下。

- It can be generalized to three-dimensional problems fairly easily.
- The numerical results are in good agreement with experimental data and other numerical solutions.

以下是几篇论文的结论部分，供大家参考。

In this article, we proposed a new phase-field model for the incompressible, immiscible ternary fluid flows with interfaces. The model consists of a Navier-Stokes equation with an extra surface tension term resulting from the presence of interfaces and a Cahn-Hilliard equation with the corresponding transport term. We used a recent chemical potential [5] and continuous surface tension force formulation [20], which has the capability to generalize to multicomponent fluid flow models. We presented several illustrative numerical examples which exhibited various physical mechanisms of the model and demonstrated its robustness and versatility. In upcoming work, we will investigate the cases with more than three-component fluid flows with surface tension. In that work, we will generalize the continuous surface tension force formulation to multicomponent (more than three) fluid flows.

A new surface tension force formulation for diffuse-interface models has been derived for incompressible, immiscible Navier-Stokes equations separated by an interface. The new formulation allows us to calculate pressure field directly from the governing equations. Numerical experiments have been presented to demonstrate the accuracy and effectiveness of the method. The results showed that the method is promising in the numerical simulation of two-phase fluid flows. In the future, we would like to incorporate adaptive mesh refinement method into the diffuse-interface method. When we solve fluid flow problems with moving interfaces numerically, high grid resolution is needed to adequately solve the equations. However, there are often also large portions of the domain where high levels of refinement are not needed; using a highly refined mesh in these regions represents a waste of computational effort. By locally refining the mesh only where needed, Adaptive Mesh Refinement(AMR) allows concentration of effort where it is needed, allowing better resolution of the problem. Fig. 16 illustrates this concept. We recursively refine the mesh around the interface to resolve interfacial area and put most of computational load on that region. Currently, we are developing AMR diffuse-interface model for an incompressible two-phase fluid flow system using the adaptive framework [1] from "The Center for Computational Sciences and Engineering at Lawrence Berkeley National Laboratory".

In this paper, an efficient and accurate numerical scheme was proposed for solving the CH equation with a variable mobility. The new scheme is solved by a nonlinear multigrid method and is second-order accurate in space and time. We have studied the dynamics of the one-, two-, and three-dimensional CH equations with a constant mobility and a compositional-dependent mobility. Particularly, we compared the kinetics of bulk-diffusion-controlled coarsening and interface-diffusion-controlled coarsening. We found, in the case of a variable mobility, after the early stages there is very little interaction of regions that do not intersect and the evolution takes place locally where the local mass is preserved. The final frame yields a numerical stationary solution consisting of many components that do not intersect. While, in the case of the constant mobility, diffusion through bulk regions is still possible and disconnected regions influence each other in order to decrease the total amount of interfacial area. For large times, constant mobility CH systems generically lead to situations where each phase occupies only one connected part of the domain.

An efficient, second order accurate finite difference scheme was used to simulate a phase-field model of the dynamics of step-flow during epitaxial growth. Step meandering and bunching was studied. Step-step interactions were seen to reduce the meandering instability. **In future work**, we will investigate the effects of edge diffusion, anisotropy and elastic interactions as these phenomena can play a critical role in step meandering and bunching instabilities [1].

We proposed the generalized continuous surface tension force (GCSF) model for surface tension for multi-component fluid flow. In the GCSF model, a surface force was formulated to model numerically the surface tension effects at fluid interfaces having finite thickness. The method is ideally suited for multi-component fluid flows. We overcame previous shortcomings on the extension to multi-component (more than three) fluid flows. The GCSF model has been validated successfully on both static and dynamic interfaces having surface tension. An important aspect of the GCSF is its generality with respect to the number of the fluid components. In general, for N component fluids, the surface tension force formulation is

$$\boldsymbol{SF}(\boldsymbol{c})=\sum_{i=1}^{N-1}\left(\sum_{j=i+1}^{N}\frac{\sigma_{ij}}{2}[\boldsymbol{sf}(c_i)+\boldsymbol{sf}(c_j)]\delta(c_i,\ c_j)\right).$$

Although this generalized surface tension force formulation was described in the context of the phase-field method, we expect that it can be useful in other methods such as the level set method. Further topics of our future research related to the presented GCSF include higher order numerical treatments and sophisticated formula to accurately recover the interfacial angles at triple points where three fluids are in contact. Also, to speed up the calculations, we will investigate an adaptive time stepping algorithm as in [10].

3.10 声明

开展研究和撰写论文需要关注的头绪很多，例如资金问题、合作者在研究中的分工，以及论文中提供的数据结果是否允许被其他论文使用等。科研诚信与学术道德非常重要，所以许多学术期刊要求声明相关内容。如果提交的论文没有相关声明，很多学术期刊会视之为不完整的论文，因此了解投稿期刊要求声明的内容很重要。本节介绍三种具有代表性的声明。

3.10.1 利益冲突声明

利益冲突声明(Conflict of Interests)或竞争利益声明(Competing Interests)是用来说明论文的主题在特定问题上是否存在利益冲突的。如果存在利益冲突，论文给出的结论可能会产生偏见，因此需要准确描述。以下是利益冲突声明的常用表述。

- The authors declare that they have no competing interests.

- The authors have no conflicts of interest to declare that are relevant to the content of this article.
- The authors declare that they have no known competing financial interests or personal relationships that could have appeared to influence the work reported in this paper.
- None.

3.10.2 作者贡献声明

合作科学研究非常普遍。有人提出想法，有人进行数值实验，有人负责撰写论文，也有很多情况下，大家的工作有交叉。因此，详细写明每个参与研究的人员的贡献是十分有必要的。有些学术期刊可能不需要作者投稿，但大多数期刊鼓励以作者身份投稿。

以下是几篇作者贡献声明的范文。

- Yang Junxiang: Conceptualization, Software, Validation, Formal analysis, Investigation, Writing-original draft, Writing-review and editing, Visualization. Lee Chaeyoung: Software, Validation, Investigation, Writing-original draft, Writing-review and editing, Visualization, Funding acquisition. Jeong Darae: Formal analysis, Investigation, Writing-original draft. Li Yibao: Conceptualization, Methodology, Software, Validation, Formal analysis, Investigation, Writing-original draft, Writing-review and editing, Supervision, Project administration, Funding acquisition.
- Li Jia researched the relevant literature, prepared the manuscript and corrected the manuscript based on suggestions from Joanne Macdonald and Fabrice Rossignol. Dr Joanne Macdonald suggested the review topic, and both Dr Joanne Macdonald and Dr Fabrice Rossignol assisted in guiding the research direction of the manuscript and editing the paper.

All authors approve of the final version of the manuscript.

- All authors contributed equally and significantly in writing this article. All authors read and approved the final manuscript.

3.10.3 数据可用性声明

论文中的数据是指能够支持论文所提出的观点并解释研究结果的所有数据。论文的读者可能需要这些数据来进行更深入的理解甚至进行后续研究。因此，论文作者需要在数据可用性部分声明数据是否可以共享。数据可用性可以分为三种情况：第一种情况，数据可部分公开。这种情况下，需要写明数据被分成几个部分，每个部分在哪里可以获取，如果可能的话，最好附上超链接。第二，不能公开获取，但可以通过有限的方式获取。如可通过个人请求获取数据，您只需要写明可以请求获取数据的条件即可，一般来说这种情况需要联系通讯作者。第三，不公开数据的情况。作者最好在论文中撰写是否公开数据的声明。

以下是几篇论文的数据可用性声明的范文。

- Our codes are available on GitHub [23].
- The data used to support the findings of this study are included within the article.
- The datasets and algorithms generated during and/or analysed during the current study are available from the corresponding author on reasonable request. Moreover, the approach presented in this paper will be included in the hm-toolbox in the near future.
- The raw data will be available based on the request to the corresponding author.
- Not applicable.

3.11 致谢

致谢通常在附录或参考文献之前。但有的期刊可能会要求对研究资助的致谢放在论文第一页的脚注中。以下是一些实例。

- This research is supported by National Natural Science Foundation of China(No. …)
- The first and second authors acknowledge the support of A.
- This research was supported by A. This research was supported by B.
- This research was supported by A. The first author was supported by B. The corresponding author was also supported by C.

在对提出论文修改意见的研究人员表示感谢时，可参考如下表述。

- The author thanks Junseok Kim for suggesting this problem and for valuable discussions regarding the energy stability of the proposed scheme.
- The authors thank Herman Frieboes, Li Yibao, and Zheng Xiaoming for many useful discussions.
- The authors would like to acknowledge fruitful conversation with our colleagues J.S.Kim, J.S.Park, and J.S.Lee.
- The authors would like to thank Professor Junseok Kim for helpful conversations on interface computations.

当您想对导师表示感谢时，可使用以下表述方式。

- The author thanks his advisor, Li Yibao, for intellectual and financial support.

如果您在论文中使用了其他研究人员的代码，您可以参考如下表述方式来表示感谢。

- We greatly appreciate Dr. Li Yibao for generously providing the multigrid code for the binary and ternary Cahn-Hilliard equations without the presence of elastic energy.
- The authors appreciate the help of Dr. Li Yibao in using the ODE solver, bvp5c.
- The authors would like to thank C. Permann (INL), J. Miller(INL), and R. H. Stogner(Univ. of Texas, Austin) for their invaluable assistance in the preparation of this manuscript.

需要注意的是，如果论文中对前人的研究结果进行了修改和订正，建议提前获得前人许可或者对论文结果有足够信心的时候再表达致谢和声明。

- The authors are indebted to John Kim for his pioneering work on the method and for helpful discussions on the use of the method in the context of IBM computations.
- We also thank the Center of Applied Scientific Computing at Lawrence Livermore National Laboratory for providing us with access to the computational resources required to perform the simulations of cardiac blood-muscle-valve mechanics.
- Li Yibao would like to acknowledge the hospitality received at Minnesota during his visit where he accomplished this work.

如果当前研究论文是基于作者个人博士论文的内容修改而来，可参考如下表述。

- This work is a part of the first author's Ph. D. thesis at Courant Institute of Mathematical Sciences, New York University.

论文最后还应对审稿人表示感谢，可参考如下表述。

- The authors thank an anonymous referee for very useful

comments on this paper.

- The authors also wish to thank the anonymous referee for the constructive and helpful comments on the revision of this article.
- The authors also wish to thank the reviewers for the constructive and helpful comments on the revision of this article.
- We thank A and B for their comments on an early version of this paper.
- I thank the reviewers. Their comments helped to improve the paper.
- We thank A, B, C, and D for stimulating discussions and for very helpful comments on the paper.
- The authors are grateful to the anonymous referees whose valuable suggestions and comments significantly improved the quality of this paper.
- The authors would also like to thank the reviewers for their contributions to improve the paper.

3.12 附录

为了帮助读者理解论文，作者可以将论文的补充内容写在附录中，并进行更详细的描述。附录一般放在论文正文和参考文献之间。对附录内容的介绍可参考以下示例。

- The Mathematica code follows with some explanations of critical steps.
- Brief details of the derivation of the finite-difference approximation (1) are given here.
- A sample MATLAB code is given in Appendix A.

3.13 参考文献

3.13.1 文后参考文献

参考文献是作者在论文撰写时所参考的论文、书籍或互联网上的相关内容。不同期刊对参考文献的格式要求有所不同，这部分内容需要仔细检查才能符合规范。一些软件（比如 Endnote、Zotero 等）可以按不同格式的要求自动生成参考文献。但为了稳妥起见，在投稿前应找来目标期刊上新近发表的几篇论文，认真比对参考文献的格式。

期刊网站主页上的参考文献格式和已发表论文中的参考文献格式可能不同。另外，在同一期刊中，参考文献格式可能会因年份而存在差异，应以最新发表的论文的格式为准。

编写参考文献时，您可以首先找到引用过您想要引用的文献的论文，在该论文的参考文献中查看引用信息，这样可以比较轻松地找到作者缩写或期刊缩写。

参考文献必须是已发表或即将发表的成果，未发表的成果或者个人交流性研究只需在正文中提及。

以下是编写参考文献的注意事项。

- 在输入来自非英语国家的作者姓名时，请参考以下输入方式。需要指出的是，此处有些是符号，不是公式。

特殊字符

ò	$\grave{o}$	ó	$\acute{o}$	ô	$\hat{o}$	õ	$\tilde{o}$
ō	$\bar{o}$	ȯ	$\dot{o}$	ö	$\ddot{o}$	$\vec{o}$	$\vec{o}$
ŏ	$\breve{o}$	ǒ	$\check{o}$	$\widehat{oo}$	$\widehat{oo}$	$\widetilde{oo}$	$\widetilde{oo}$
o̧	\c{o}	ő	\H{o}	ọ	\d{o}		
œ	\oe	Œ	\OE	æ	\ae	Æ	\AE

- 确认是否按期刊格式标注作者姓名。
- 注意列举三位作者时的格式，A, B, and C 或 A, B and C。
- 期刊名称的缩写使用是否正确。
- 在复制和粘贴其他论文的参考文献时，页码可能显示乱码，比如：123? 456。因此复制内容时请注意检查。
- 参考文献列表是否按第一作者姓名字母顺序排列，或者是按照正文中引用的顺序排序。
- 检查所投期刊的论文是否在参考文献中。这可以间接衡量一篇论文是否适合该期刊。

3.13.2 正文中引用文献的常用表述方式

标注引文数据来源的原因包括：通过揭示引文来源，认可其他研究人员的贡献；告知读者论文中所引用事实的准确性；向读者呈现作为研究背景的文献数据；帮助读者复现或深化这些文献的研究内容。文献中有一到两位作者时，一般标注所有作者的姓名，并且作者名字之间用 and 进行连接；当有三位及以上作者时，仅使用第一作者的姓和“et al.”进行标注。

- Some approaches are presented by Yamada [3], Abate and Whitt [1], and Ata et al. [2].
- As was shown by Fife [1], the Allen-Cahn Equation is gradient flow for E(u) in the L2 inner product. The main reason for including in this paper is the essential role that it plays in the study of partial differential equations.

直接引用已发表论文可使用以下表述方式。

- In our previous work [1], we introduced the concept.
- It should be noted that the numerical scheme used in this paper has previously been employed in [1]. However, to the

best of our knowledge, this particular numerical scheme had not previously been applied to the CH equation.

- In [1], the authors showed that their genetic algorithm was practically useful.

引用参考文献时,应避免引用那些您并没有理解的论文,因为这会让读者在阅读时感到失望甚至被欺骗。要特别注意的是,引用最近发表的论文很重要,同时也需要非常审慎,因为这些论文的作者可能是就是你的论文的审稿人。

当被要求参阅参考书目和参考资料时,可参考如下示例。

- For recent reviews of phase-field methods, the reader is referred to [1,2,3].
- Please refer to [1] for more details.
- A review on integral models can be found in [1].
- See reference [2] and references therein.
- See reference [2] and references cited therein.
- For more details on the thin film equations, see the review paper [1] and references therein.
- For a survey of earlier work on equation (1) we refer to [1, 2,3] and to the literature cited therein.

4 提交论文

提交论文时，上传的稿件必须是最终版本，确保完整。作者应根据论文的研究方向选择最合适的期刊。提交论文时的注意事项有以下几点。

- 不要将同一篇论文同时提交给多个期刊。
- 论文的所有参与作者都必须同意投稿。
- 必须得到作者所在的公司、研究机构或学校的同意。
- 对于之前已经发布过的图片，必须获得发布者的许可。

您应该仔细选择要投稿的期刊。在选择目标期刊时，请考虑以下因素。

- 论文主题、论文类型等是否符合目标期刊的方向。
- 是否为权威期刊。
- 是否为引用率(影响因子)高的期刊。
- 论文审查期是否较长。
- 是否有投稿费和出版费(一定要查)。
- 期刊文章格式。
- 只开放获取的期刊，发表率相对较高。

这里给大家分享一个查找目标期刊的网站：http://

journalfinder. elsevier. com/。

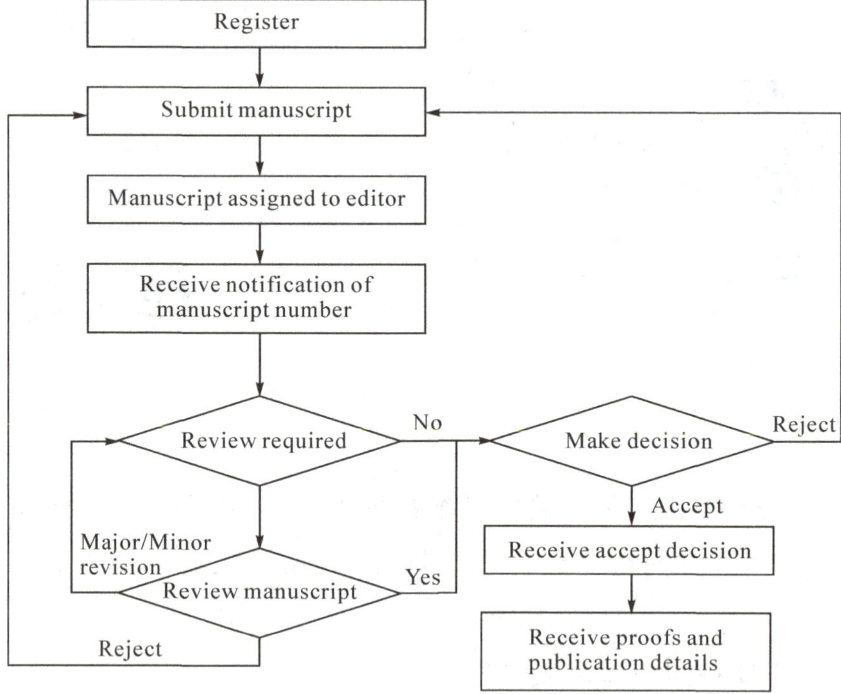

图 4-2 论文投稿及审稿过程

电气与电子工程师协会(IEEE)的期刊使用以下标准来评估论文的质量。

- Is the topic appropriate for publication in these transactions?
- Is the topic important to colleagues working in the field?
- Is the paper technically sound?
- Is the coverage of the topic sufficiently comprehensive and balanced?
- How would you describe technical depth of paper?
- How would you rate the technical novelty of the paper?
- How would you rate the overall organization of the paper?
- Are the title and abstract satisfactory?

- Is the length of the paper appropriate? If not, recommend how the length of the paper should be amended, including a possible target length for the final manuscript. Are symbols, terms, and concepts adequately defined?
- How do you rate the English usage?
- Rate the Bibliography.
- How would you rate the technical contents of the paper?
- How would you rate the novelty of the paper?
- How would you rate the "literary" presentation of the paper?
- How would you rate the appropriateness of this paper for publication in this IEEE Transactions?

4.1 投稿信

规范得体的投稿信不仅能让论文获得更多关注，还可能提高论文送审概率。建议将投稿信与论文手稿一起发送。如果有多个作者，请写明通讯作者的地址。此外，投稿信中还应阐述论文中最重要的发现、研究的创新点、研究对知识世界的贡献等。编辑将对他们提交的论文更感兴趣。以下是投稿信的参考例文。

Cover Letter

July 14, 2009
Journal A
Dear Editor:

Please consider the manuscript entitled "A numerical method for the Cahn-Hilliard equation" authored by Li Yibao which I am submitting for consideration for publication in Journal A. This manuscript is new and is not being considered elsewhere.

Sincerely,
Li Yibao
Professor
Department of Mathematics
Xi'an Jiaotong University

以下是合著论文的投稿信参考例文。

Cover Letter

July 14, 2009
Journal A
Dear Editor:

Please consider the manuscript entitled "A numerical method for the Cahn-Hilliard equation" authored by Li Yibao and Dong Hongli which we are submitting for consideration for publication in Journal A. This manuscript is new and is not being considered elsewhere.

Sincerely,
Li Yibao
Professor
Department of Mathematics
Xi'an Jiaotong University

4.2 选择审稿人

通常，投稿时应提供 3～8 位审稿人的名单。推荐论文审稿人时应考虑其是否对该领域比较熟悉，比如近 10 年内发表过该领域的论文。

最好从您的参考文献目录中选择审稿人。此外，请务必提前确认审稿人的电子邮件地址和所在机构。您推荐的审稿人越多，论文处理速度就越快。但请注意确认审稿人的推荐人数量是否有限制。在撰写推荐理由时，请使用审稿人的姓名，而不是"他"或"她"这样的字眼。比如：LI Yibao is an expert in this research area.。

审稿是对学术界的一项服务。就像我们希望其他研究人员审阅我们提交的论文一样，如果对方提交的论文是有创新性的，也是按照相关规范书写的，审阅投稿人的论文应该被视为学术界的一种礼仪。

4.3 技术检查

论文提交之后，如果您未按期刊规定撰写论文，期刊主编可能会给您发送以下邮件。

Thank you for submitting your work to Journal ABC.

Before we pass on manuscripts to the Journal Editor, who is responsible for the scientific assessment, we perform an initial check against formal technical criteria (structure of submission, adherence to the Guide for Authors and English language usage). We regret to inform you that your manuscript does not meet the journal's required standard for the reasons detailed in the comments below.

You are welcome to resubmit your manuscript. Should you do so, please ensure that every aspect of the manuscript is in accordance with the Guide for Authors. You must also submit a separate list of responses to the problems that were raised, under the submission item "Responses to technical check results". We regret that without a completed "Responses" sheet, your manuscript will not be further processed.

PLEASE NOTE: resubmission is not a guarantee that your paper will subsequently proceed to the peer review process, which is a decision to be made at the sole discretion of the Editor. Yours sincerely, Comments:

1) Full contact addresses of only 3-5 potential reviewers including their e-mail addresses should be provided.

2) Graphical abstract should be structured under the heading "Graphical abstract".

针对以上邮件提出的问题，可以参照以下邮件内容给期刊回信，并重新在线提交您的论文。

<JOURNAL TITLE>

<MANUSCRIPT TITLE>

Dear editor,

Thank you for your useful comments and suggestions on the language and the structure of our manuscript. We have modified the manuscript accordingly, and the detailed corrections are listed below point by point:

1) Full contact addresses of only 3-5 potential reviewers including their e-mail addresses should be provided.

We suggested 5 potential reviewers including their e-mail addresses.

2) Graphical abstract should be structured under the heading "Graphical abstract".

We corrected a graphical abstract that structured under the heading "Graphical abstract".

The manuscript has been resubmitted to your journal. We look forward to your positive response.

<Signature>

4.4 修改论文

论文在被接收后,审稿人可能会要求作者进行修改。如果是小修的情况,可以尽快修改并回复审稿意见。但如果是大修的情况,则需要花更多的时间仔细修改,一般在一个月内回复为宜。如果回复审稿意见不及时,之前的审稿人可能会拒绝论文审稿。在这种情况下,论文审稿可能会被延迟。

4.4.1 修改稿附信

以下是修改稿附信的例文。

Cover Letter

July 14, 2022

Journal A

Dear Editor:

According to reviewers' comments, we have revised our manuscript. We have enclosed the responses (which summarize the revisions and corrections) to reviewers.

We are looking forward to hearing from you.

Sincerely,

Li Yibao

Full Professor

Department of Mathematics

Xi'an Jiaotong University

4.4.2 回复审稿意见

收到审稿和返修意见后，您应该根据审稿人的意见尽快进行修改，并撰写一封邮件，说明修改的情况。审稿人可能不记得之前审稿提出的所有问题，所以回信时先写审稿人的问题（Q），然后再写自己的解释（A）。

以下例文供大家参考。

Reply Letter

November 5, 2009

Journal A

Dear Editor and Reviewer:

Thank you so much for reviewing my manuscript and useful comments. We are submitting the revised version of our manuscript. We gave point by point responses of all the comments made by the reviewers.

Q. On the other hand, the gyromagnetic term in the LL equation is a conservative term. Therefore, any reliable numerical method for the LL equation without damping and with zero Neumann data must be compliant with this property. The authors offer numerical evidence of this result (Section 3), but a proof is not provided. Further, the authors claim that their numerical method is second order, but only numerical evidence is offered.

A. We provided proofs of the conservations of the magnitude and energy and the second order accuracy of the numerical method in new Section 2.2 in the revised paper.

The authors'contact information is yibaoli@xjtu.edu.cn.

Sincerely,

Li Yibao

Professor

Department of Mathematics

Xi'an Jiaotong University

4.5 催稿或撤稿

4.5.1 催稿邮件

投交论文后如果较长时间未收到回复，或投稿系统上状态未更新，可给编辑发送邮件询问情况。以下是两篇邮件例文，供大家参考。

Dear <u>Editor's name</u>,

<u>Title of your manuscript</u>

It is more than six months since we submitted the above mentioned manuscript to you for possible publication in Journal A. We would like to know what is the current status of our manuscript. The manuscript number is AAAA01234567.

We are looking forward to your reply.

Thank you.

Sincerely yours,

Li Yibao

Dear Editor's name,

We submitted the manuscript AAAA01234567 entitled "BBBBBBB" for publication in Journal A as an original paper in June 21, 2022.

Today we checked that current status/date of the manuscripts has not been changed since we initially submitted the manuscript. We would like to know the current status of the manuscript.

We look forward to hearing from you.

Sincerely yours,

Li Yibao

发送提醒邮件后，如需要确认对方是否收到邮件，可以加上一句 Please kindly acknowledge receipt of this e-mail.。

4.5.2 撤稿邮件

如果认为审稿周期过长或者审稿过程未进行，也可以申请撤回文章。以下是参考例文。

Dear Editor

We wish to withdraw our manuscript because it took so long time since we submitted our manuscript. The manuscript number is AAAA01234567.

We are looking forward to your reply.

Thank you.

Sincerely yours,

Li Yibao

以下是期刊编辑部针对以上邮件的回复。

Title: AAAA01234567-Confirmation of manuscript being officially

Ref: AAAA01234567 Title: BBBBBBBB

Dear Prof. Li

I want to confirm that your submitted manuscript is now considered to be withdrawn, and its record in the online system is now closed.

Pattern Recognition

发送邮件后,您可以请求回执确认。常用表述如下。

- Please acknowledge receipt of this message.
- Kindly acknowledge receipt to of this e-mail.
- Please acknowledge receipt of this e-mail.

4.6 论文投稿流程

论文投稿是论文正式发表之前必须经历的阶段。投稿之后,期刊主编会根据论文的主题将其分给相关领域的审稿人。多个审稿人进行同行评议之后,会给出相应的专业性意见,作者需要根据该论文收到的评审意见针对文章进行相应的修改,使得该论文达到期刊的发表要求。不同的出版社投稿要求不同。我们以爱思唯尔出版社(Elsevier)为例,针对投稿过程进行相应的说明。

第一步：注册相应期刊的账号。通常使用机构邮箱来注册，并设定相应的密码登录期刊系统，点击 Submit your article。

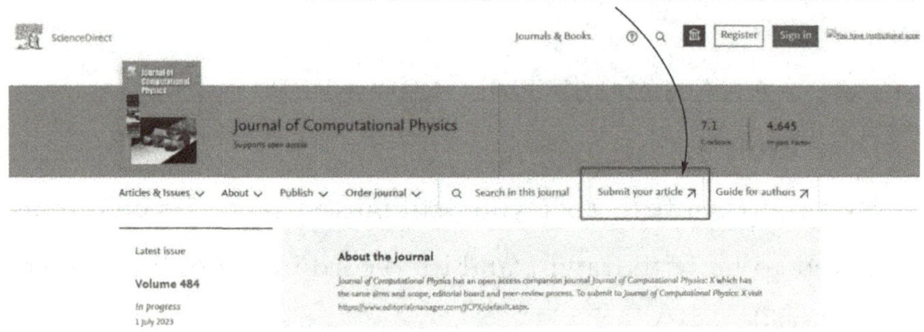

第二步：输入相应的账号和密码。

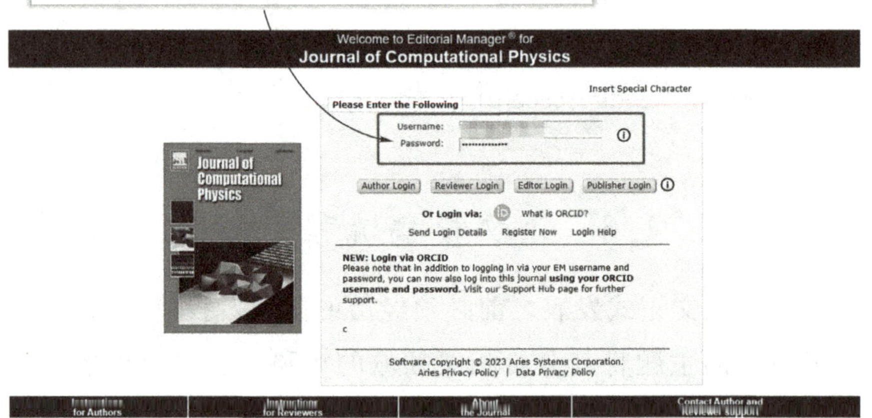

第三步：点击 Submit New Manuscript。

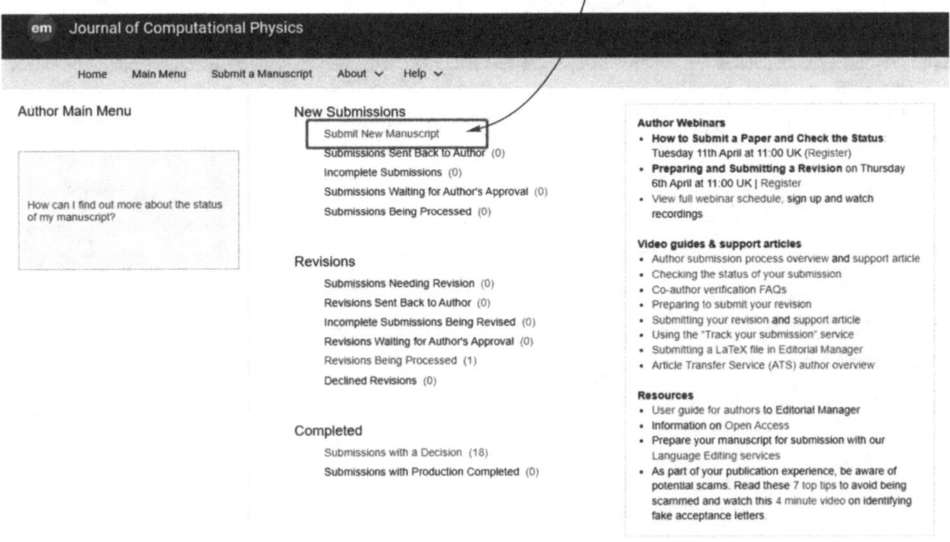

第四步：选择投稿的文章类型，包括 Regular Article、Short Note、Letter to the Editor 等选项。

第五步：将论文投稿所准备的所有文件整合到一个压缩包中，点击 Browse，上传该压缩包。

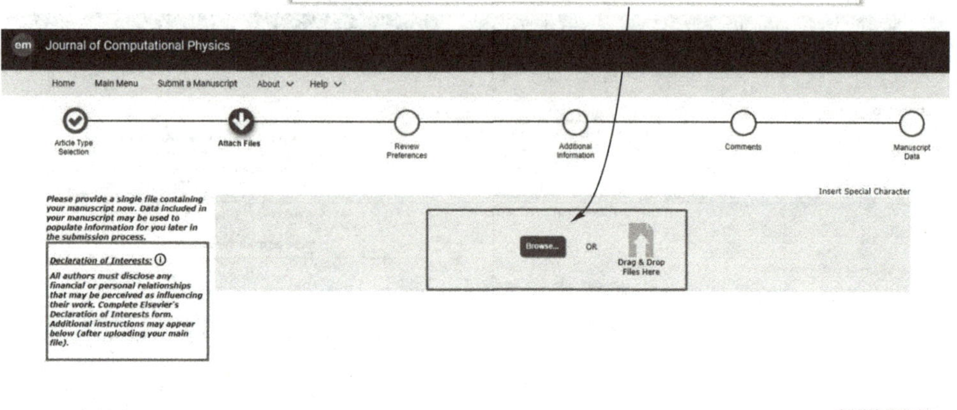

第六步：上传必备文件并按顺序进行整理。

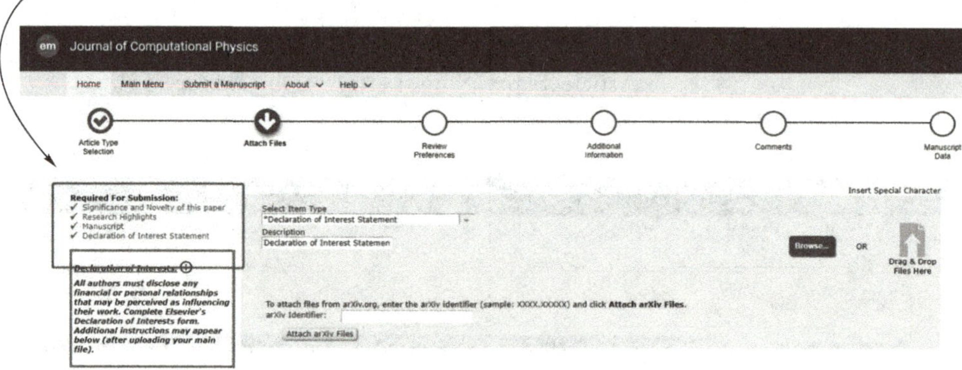

第七步：推荐编辑。如对编辑没有要求就选择 No Request。

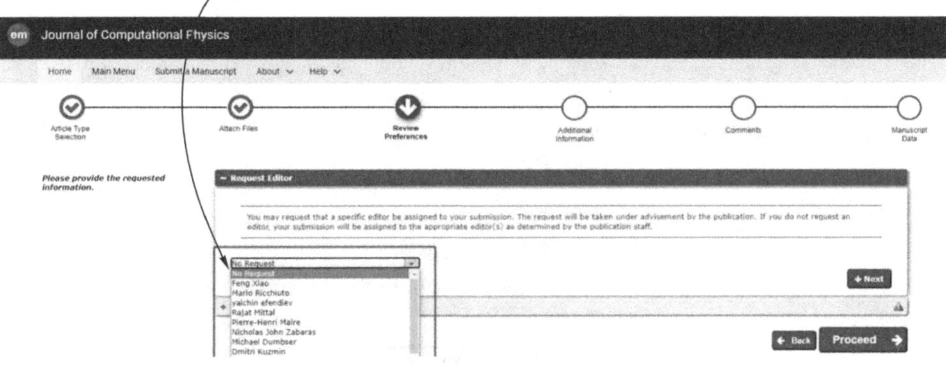

第八步：建议选择 3 个审稿人，最好是同一个领域的专家。

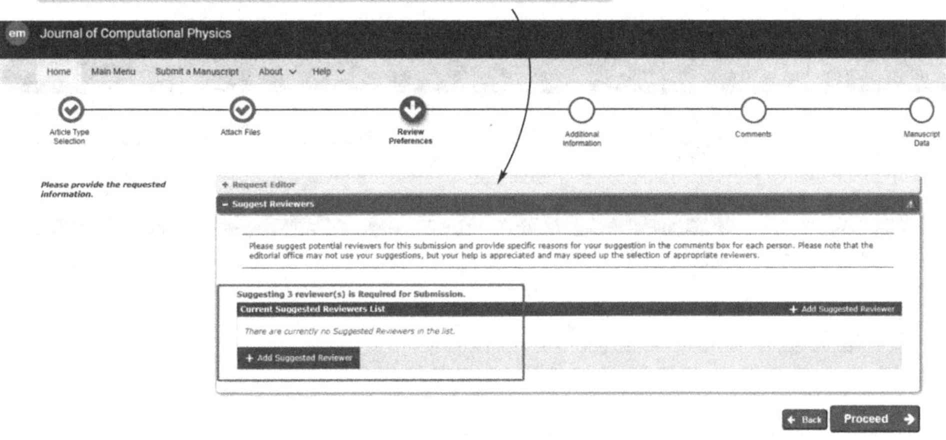

第九步：通常要写清楚建议审稿人的名字、单位、邮箱地址，以及选择他或她作为审稿人的原因。

Add New Reviewer

Insert Special Characters

Given/First Name *	xx
Middle Name	
Family/Last Name *	xx
Degree	
Position	
Institution	XX University Start typing to display potentially matching institutions.
Department	
E-mail *	xx@xx.edu.cn
Reason	XX is the expert in this field.

第十步：进入 Additional Information 部分，可根据论文情况选择相应的回复。

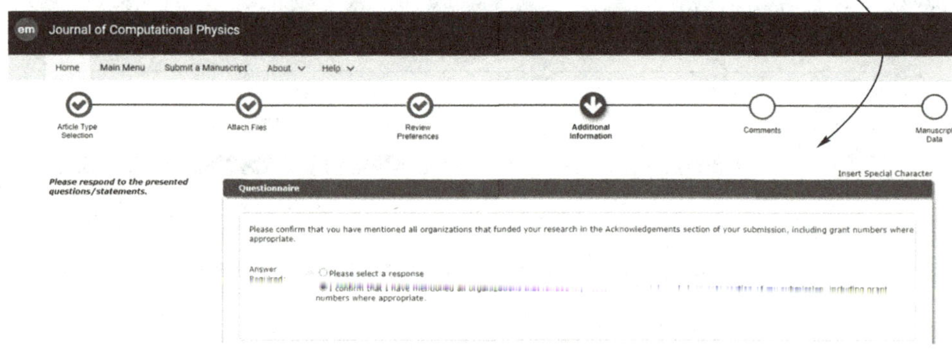

第十一步：进入 Comments 部分，针对该论文向编辑部进行简短的、总结性的介绍。

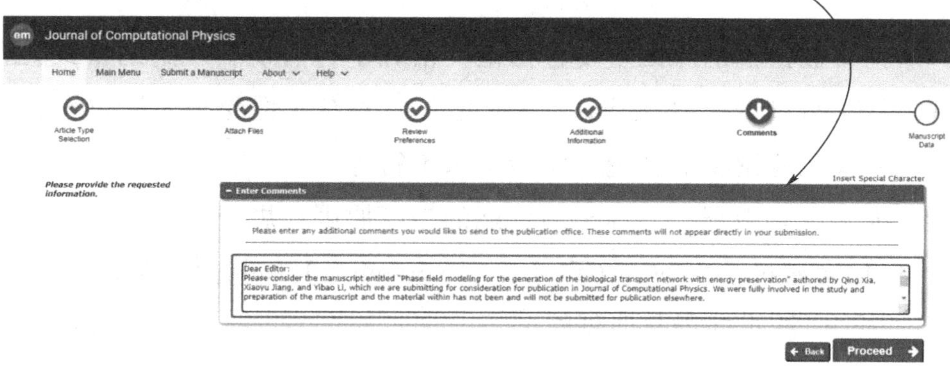

第十二步：针对论文的部分细节问题进行相应的补充。分别填上标题、摘要、关键词、作者、基金资助等信息，完成之后，点击 Build PDF for Approval，在系统中生成相应的投稿文件，查看无误后点击提交。

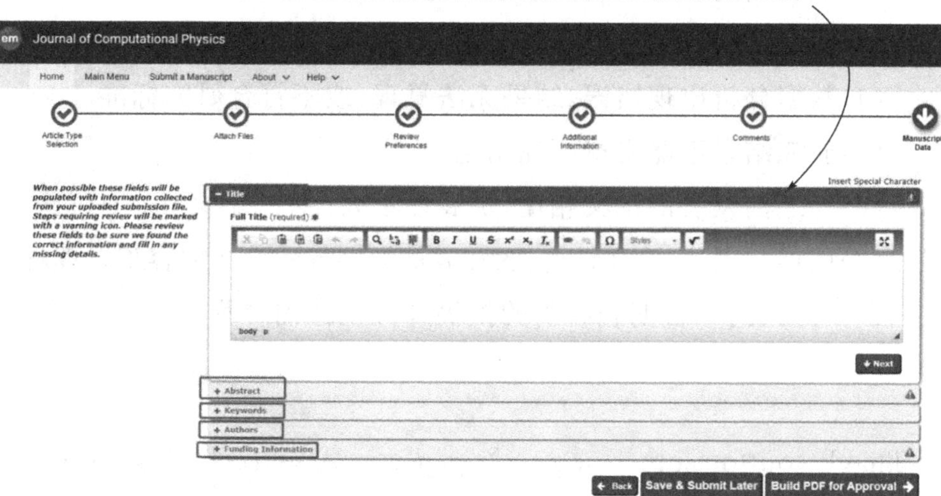

4.7 拒稿

论文被拒稿的原因主要包括论文格式不符合期刊规定的格式，出现多处拼写错误或语法错误，使研究人员的专业性受到质疑，论文没有创新性或者论文的结论与实验结果不符等。

大家可以根据下面列出的可能的拒稿原因反思个人的论文。

(1)未通过技术筛选（Technical screening），编辑直接拒稿。

- 涉嫌抄袭其他稿件。
- 文稿不完整，例如没有标题、作者姓名、单位地址、关键词、参考文献、表格和图形等。
- 英文表述混乱，无法进行同行评审。
- 图片不完整且不清晰。
- 稿件不符合投稿期刊的规范。
- 参考文献不完整或参考文献太陈旧。

(2)该文稿内容与期刊的主题和范围不符。

(3)研究结果不完整或不充分。

(4)数据分析出现错误，结果无法复现，或不符合研究标准。

(5)研究结果不能支撑研究结论。

(6)与之前发表的论文相比，扩展性不大。

(7)因英文表达、论文结构、图和表等原因导致论文内容难以理解。

以下是两封来自期刊编辑的拒稿邮件主体内容示例。

Thank you for submitting your paper to A journal. The pre-review process has now been completed. It has been found that, unfortunately, the paper is not appropriate for this journal. We believe that the material presented would be much more appreciated in a mathematics oriented journal. Consequently, I suggest that you resubmit your paper to a more appropriate publishing medium. Thank you for your interest in and support of A journal.

We have examined your paper, and conclude that it is not suitable for this Journal. It is our consensus that a specialized journal in this area would bring your paper to the attention of a more interested audience. This is not a judgment on the technical quality of your manuscript.

5 注意英文表达

要时刻谨记，哪怕论文很有创新性，但如果其中有大量不符合规范的英语表达和语法错误，会影响审稿人对论文的印象，也很可能会被拒稿。特别需要强调的是，已发表的论文中也可能有语法错误，要注意辨别。下面我们结合学术论文写作来看一些具体例子。

5.1 冠词

冠词分为不定冠词和定冠词，其用法比较灵活。

5.1.1 不定冠词 a 和 an

不定冠词一般表示“一个”的含义。注意 a 和 an 的选择是根据后面单词的发音来确定的，而不是根据其拼写来确定的。比如：

(1)an 用于元音音素开头的元音字母前。

- **an** MRI scan, **an** hour, **an** honest boy, **an** N, **an** honor

(2)a 用于以辅音音素开头的辅音字母前。

- **a** UV light, **a** one-dimensional space, **a** useful tool, **a** uniform grid, in **a** unified way, **a** European option

5.1.2 定冠词 the

定冠词主要用法举例如下。

(1)the 放在前文已经出现的名词之前。

- A three-dimensional computer model has been developed to simulate fluid flow. **The** model is based on the immersed boundary method.
- A method is proposed for computing material defect and surface properties accurately at the atomic level. **The** method is both simple and accurate and treats both semiconductors and metals.

(2)the 可以用来表示特指。

- We propose a new algorithm. **The** accuracy of the proposed algorithm is demonstrated by test problems.

(3)the 用在序数词之前。

- **The** second step then uses the results of **the** first step.

(4)the 用在最高级之前。

- From the linear stability analysis, **the** fastest growing mode is approximately given by $k = 7$.

5.1.3 冠词的省略

章节标题中的第一个冠词一般可省略。此外,图和表格的标题也要省略第一个冠词。有时介词 with 或者 of 之后的冠词可省略。比如:

- The random variables were generated from a normal distribution **with zero expectation**.
- We shall now obtain the equation **of motion** for p.
- The velocity **of propagation** is a function of the diameter of the rod.

5.2 动词的单数和复数

动词要与主语一致，具体举例如下。

- The number of time steps is $Nt = 100$.
- A number of applications of the method have been described in the literature.
- The behavior of stratified flows has been studied experimentally.(flows 不是主语，The behavior 才是主语)
- Each of these samples was analyzed five times.

5.3 时态的一致性

时态的一致性是指主句中的动词时态一般应与从句中的动词时态保持一致。

- The results demonstrated that the proposed method produced higher quality solutions with faster convergence.
- The average life span of bees in our experiment was 8 weeks.

但当从句陈述的内容是一般性真理时，这种情况下主句和从句的时态可能不一致。

- The results demonstrated that the heat transfer performance increases with increasing Reynolds number.

5.4 注意事项

以下是英文论文写作中的一些注意事项。

(1)不使用缩略形式。

正式写作中不应出现 it's、isn't、weren't、can't、don't 等缩略形式。

(2)And 或 But 不应出现在句首。

在句首可以使用 Furthermore 来代替 And 表示并列。用 However 来代替 But，表示转折。

(3)专有名词注意大小写。

人名或其他专有名词首字母应大写，例如 Jacobian matrix 或 Euler's method。

(4)使用代词，避免重复。

使用指示代词可以使表达更加凝练，也比较符合英文的表述习惯。具体例子如下。

- The Cahn-Hilliard equation with a variable mobility is computationally more costly then **that** with a constant mobility.
- The Cahn-Hilliard equations with a variable mobility are computationally more costly then **those** with a constant mobility.
- Our results are consistent with **those** of Evans et al. [1].

5.5 常见错误及修改方式

在英文写作中，有时会出现词语顺序不当、搭配错误、时态误用等情况。以下是一些英文论文写作中常见错误的举例及其正确用法。

- Typical chromatographic patterns obtained under **the described above condition** are shown in Fig. 1.

改为：Typical chromatographic patterns obtained under **the condition described above** are shown in Fig. 1.

- The synchronized state is stable if **the both conditions** (1) and (2) are satisfied.

改为：The synchronized state is stable if **both the conditions** (1) and (2) are satisfied.

• **The obtained solution** was indeed optimal.

改为：**The solution obtained** was indeed optimal.

• **The mentioned algorithm** is iterated until a certain criterion is met.

改为：**The algorithm mentioned** is iterated until a certain criterion is met.

或 **The above-mentioned algorithm** is iterated until a certain criterion is met.

• **At first**, note that our assumptions imply that r ⩾ 1.

改为：**First**, note that our assumptions imply that r ⩾ 1.

• **At last**, we conclude with a summary of the results and comments on future work.

改为：**Finally**, we conclude with a summary of the results and comments on future work.

• All other parameters are the same as described in **the Section 3**.

改为： All other parameters are the same as described in **Section 3**.

• The computational domain is schematically illustrated **on Fig. 1**.

改为：The computational domain is schematically illustrated **in Fig. 1**.

• After one cycle, **as it is shown in Fig. 1**, the dislocation positions are all within one percent of the original positions.

改为：After one cycle, **as is shown in Fig. 1**, the dislocation positions are all within one percent **of** the original positions.

• This behavior is **similar as** that of compressible mixing layers.

改为：This behavior **is similar to** that of compressible mixing layers.

- In an incompressible flow, mass conservation **is equivalent with** conservation of volume.

改为：In an incompressible flow, mass conservation **is equivalent to** conservation of volume.

- The stochastic volatility **is independent on** the stock price.

改为：The stochastic volatility **is independent of** the stock price.

- Equation (1) can be equivalently represented as the following equation by linearization using **the Taylor's formula** around the origin.

改为：Equation (1) can be equivalently represented as the following equation by linearization using **Taylor's formula** around the origin.

或　Equation (1) can be equivalently represented as the following equation by linearization using **the Taylor formula** around the origin.

- In 1905, Einstein **has showed** that light is made up of discrete wave packets, which can be seen as analogues of particles.

改为：In 1905, Einstein **showed** that light is made up of discrete wave packets, which can be seen as analogues of particles.

5.6 使用派生词

英文论文写作中使用派生词可以使表达更加丰富。具体示例如下。

- **Depending on** the initial conditions, the algorithm may converge rapidly or slowly, or may even diverge.

- To ensure **independence from** the initial flow conditions, all results shown below are those obtained at $t = 10000\Delta t$.

6 学术演讲

学术演讲是研究者分享学术成果，与同行交流的重要形式。研究者应在进行学术演讲前作好充足的准备。

学术演讲时可能会使用幻灯片。幻灯片应简洁明了，只包含与主题相关的内容。可以把自己的演讲录下来，反复回看，不断调整。肢体语言在英语演讲中也很重要，应体现出自信和从容的状态，国际学术交流中多用英语，平时应注意练习发音，还要特别注意技术术语，尤其是希腊字母或单词和拉丁字母或单词的发音。

您需要很好地管理您的演示时间。在实际演示之前进行应足够次数的排练。单独练习时，对着镜子也是一个很有效的方法。另外，将自己的演讲过程拍摄下来，反复观看您的演示过程，这也很有帮助。最好不使用脚本就能记住演示内容，以防在放映幻灯片时忘记演示内容。

让我们通过以下的演讲场景来学习如何用英语进行口头演讲。

Automatic Algorithm for Image Segmentation

Department of Mathematics, Korea University
Junseok Kim

Collaborators: HyunGeun Lee, Darae Jeong, and Dongsun Lee

MEMO

I'm a graduate student at Xi'an Jiaotong University majoring in mathematics. My name is Li Yibao. Today, I'd like to talk about automatic algorithm for image segmentation. This work was done in collaboration with HyunGeun Lee, Darae Jung, and Dongsun Lee. If you have any questions, please feel free to interrupt. The objective of my research is to remove noise in images by using a mathematical model. Left figure is a fingerprint with noise and the right figure is the fingerprint after removing the noise.

Governing equation for image segmentation

- **Mumford-Shah energy functional :**

$$\mathcal{E}(\phi) = \int_{\Omega} \left(\frac{F(\phi)}{\epsilon^2} + \frac{|\nabla \phi|^2}{2} + G(\phi, f_0) \right) d\mathbf{x}.$$

$$F(\phi) = 0.25(\phi^2 - 1)^2$$

- **Governing equation :**

$$\phi_t = -\frac{F'(\phi)}{\epsilon^2} + \Delta\phi + \lambda[(1-\phi)(f_0 - c_2)^2 - (1+\phi)(f_0 - c_1)^2].$$

MEMO

The governing equation for image segmentation can be derived from Mumford Shah energy functional. In this functional, F of phi is a fourth-order polynomial as shown in this graph. By applying the gradient descent method, we have the governing equation for image segmentation.

Proposed numerical method

- **Operator splitting technique**

Step 1) $$\phi_{ij}^{n+1,1} = e^{-\lambda[(f_0-c_1^n)^2+(f_0-c_2^n)^2]\Delta t}\phi_{ij}^n + (e^{-\lambda[(f_0-c_1^n)^2+(f_0-c_2^n)^2]\Delta t} - 1)\frac{(f_0-c_1^n)^2-(f_0-c_2^n)^2}{(f_0-c_1^n)^2+(f_0-c_2^n)^2}.$$

Step 2) $$\frac{\phi^{n+1,2}-\phi^{n+1,1}}{\Delta t} = \Delta_d\phi^{n+1,2},$$

Step 3) $$\phi^{n+1} = \frac{\phi^{n+1,2}}{\sqrt{e^{\frac{-2\Delta t}{\epsilon^2}} + (\phi^{n+1,2})^2(1-e^{\frac{-2\Delta t}{\epsilon^2}})}}.$$

if $|\phi^n| \le 1$, then we get $|\phi^{n+1}| \le 1$.

Unconditionally stable scheme !!

MEMO

The proposed numerical method is based on operator splitting technique. Here, we take three steps to advance the numerical solution from time n to time $n+1$. And this method is an unconditionally stable scheme. -Question (raise your hand): What does it mean by unconditionally stable scheme? -Answer: Okay, that is a good question. She asked "What does it mean by unconditionally stable scheme?" The unconditionally stable scheme means the existence of the numerical solution does not depend on the time step size. Does that answer your question?

Convergence test

Initial profile : $c(x,0)=\frac{1}{2}\left(1-\tanh\frac{x}{2\sqrt{2}\epsilon}\right)$

Analytic final profile : $c(x,T)=\frac{1}{2}\left(1-\tanh\frac{x-0.5}{2\sqrt{2}\epsilon}\right)$

Parameters are used as : $h=2^{1-n}, \epsilon=0.015, s=3/(\sqrt(2)\epsilon),$
$\Delta t=h/(40s), T=1/(2s).$

Case	128	rate	256	rate	512	rate	1024
$\|\mathbf{e}^{N_t}\|_2$	1.320E-2	1.972	3.363E-3	1.977	8.544E-4	1.962	2.193E-4
$\|\mathbf{e}^{N_t}\|_\infty$	5.334E-2	1.962	1.370E-2	1.975	3.486E-3	1.961	8.953E-4

☞ **second order accurate in space and time**

MEMO

Now, in order to validate the proposed numerical method, we performed the convergence test. From the table, we can observe that this method is second order accurate in space and time.

Image segmentation for a fingerprint

Parameters are used as : $\epsilon_3, \Delta t = 5E\text{-}6, tol = 0.25, \lambda = 1.5E5$ on $\Omega = (0,1) \times (0,1)$ with a 256×256 mesh.

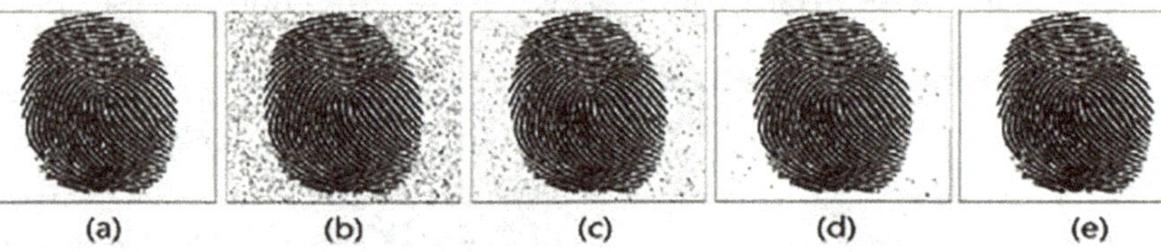

(a) (b) (c) (d) (e)

Figure 1. Temporal evolutions of a fingerprint : (a) initial image, (b) image with noise, numerical results after (c) 2 iterations, (d) 4 iterations, and (e) 10 iterations.

MEMO

To test our proposed algorithm, we took a clean image of a fingerprint (indicate image (a) with a laser point). Then, we artificially added some noise in the image (indicate image (b) with a laser point). (b) is the initial condition in our algorithm. (c), (d), and (e) are the results after 2, 4, and 10 iterations. From Figure (e), we removed most of the noise after 10 iterations.

Summary

- We proposed an unconditionally stable hybrid numerical scheme for image segmentation.
- We performed the numerical test with noisy fingerprint image.
- In our future work, we will study an automatic decision of the range of λ.

$$\phi_t = -\frac{F'(\phi)}{\epsilon^2} + \Delta\phi$$
$$+\lambda[(1-\phi)(f_0-c_2)^2 - (1+\phi)(f_0-c_1)^2].$$

MEMO

Let me summarize my talk. In this study, we proposed an unconditionally stable hybrid scheme for image segmentation. And we performed the numerical test with noisy fingerprint images. In our future work, we will study an automatic decision of the range of lambda.

MEMO

Thank you for your attention.

附录

论文投稿前必须核查的细节

检查(√)	内 容
□	论文的目的是否明确?
□	论文中引用的格式和内容是否正确?
□	参考文献是否按字母顺序或引用顺序排序?
□	正文中引用多个参考文献时标注是否准确、清晰?
□	致谢部分是否无误?
□	作者姓名拼写是否无误?
□	通讯作者是否进行了标记?
□	作者的工作单位信息是否准确、完整?
□	检查论文中是否存在单词拼写错误?
□	是否解释了所有的图片?
□	是否解释了所有的表格?
□	参考文献中期刊名称的缩写是否正确?
□	参考文献中是否有拟投稿期刊的论文?
□	投稿信中拟投稿期刊名称是否书写正确?
□	参考文献的大小写及正斜体是否准确?
□	表达式、图片和表格中是否存在重复标签?
□	公式中是否遗漏了等号?

检查(√)	内容
□	投稿信中是否阐明了论文的创新性和研究意义?
□	论文是否已经进行过重复率的检查?
□	摘要中是否包含了论文的关键内容?
□	论文中是否存在口语化的表达?
□	作者的电话号码、传真号码和地址是否正确?
□	是否需要准备文章要点和图形摘要?
□	图片文件是否按顺序进行编码?
□	如论文是在作者学位论文基础上修改、扩充而成,在致谢中是否进行了相应的说明?
□	是否提交的是论文的最新版本?
□	如果论文的内容曾在以前的会议上发表时,是否在致谢中附上了相应的说明?
□	是否依据实际情况,撰写了利益冲突声明?
□	有没有重复定义符号的情况?
□	论文文本的行距是否合适?
□	选择投稿的期刊是否合适?

参考文献

[1] B. G. Dellaert, T. A. Arentze, M. Bierlaire, A. W. Borgers, H. J. Timmermans, Investigating consumers' tendency to combine multiple shopping purposes and destinations. *Journal of Marketing Research*, 1998, 177－188.

[2] J. B. Bell, P. Colella, H. M. Glaz, A second-order projection method for the incompressible Navier－Stokes equations, *Journal of Computational Physics*, Vol. 85, 1989, 257－283.

[3] D. L. Brown, R. Cortez, M. L. Minion, Accurate projection methods for the incompressible Navier-Stokes equations, *Journal of Computational Physics*, Vol. 168, 2001, 464－499.

[4] H. Bulut, O. Kelesoglu, Comparing numerical methods for response of beams with moving mass, *Journal of Advances in Engineering Software*, Vol. 41.7, 2010, 976－980.

[5] M. Benes, K. Mikula, T. Oberhuber, and D. Sevcovic, Comparison study for Level set and Direct Lagrangian methods for computing Willmore flow of closed planar curves, *Journal of Computing and visualization in science*, Vol. 12(6), 2009, 307－317.

[6] L. Q. Chen, Phase-field models for microstructure evolution, *Annual Review of Materials Research*, Vol. 32.1, 2002, 113－140.

[7] M. Droske, W. Ring, M. Rumpf, Mumford-Shah based registration: a comparison of a level set and a phase field approach, *Computing and Visualization in Science*, Vol. 12.3, 2009, 101－114.

[8] E. Maitre, C. Misbah, P. Peyla, A. Raoult, Comparison between advected-field and level-set methods in the study of vesicle dynamics, *Physica D: Nonlinear Phenomena*, 2012.

[9] E. Javierre, C. Vuik, F. J. Vermolen, S. Van der Zwaag, A comparison of numerical models for one-dimensional Stefan problems, *Computational and Applied Mathematics*, Vol. 192(2), 2006, 445－459.

[10] D. Jeong, J. Kim, A Crank-Nicolson scheme for the Landau-Lifshitz equation without damping, *Computational and Applied Mathematics*, Vol. 234, 2010, 613–623.

[11] J. Kim, P. Moin, Application of a fractional-step method to incompressible Navier-Stokes equations, *Journal of Computational Physics*, Vol. 59, 1985, 308–323.

[12] J. Kim, A numerical method for the Cahn-Hilliard equation with a variable mobility, *Communications in Nonlinear Science and Numerical Simulation*, Vol. 12, 2007, 1560–1571.

[13] J. Kim, Numerical simulations of phase separation dynamics in a water-oil-surfactant system, *Journal of Colloid and Interface Science*, Vol. 303, 2006, 272–279.

[14] H. Liu, Y. Zhang, Phase-field modeling droplet dynamics with soluble surfactants, *Journal of Computational Physics*, Vol. 229, 2010, 9166–9187.

[15] M. Peric, R. Kessler, G. Scheuerer, Comparison of finite-volume numerical methods with staggered and colocated grids, *Computers and Fluids*, Vol. 16.4, 1988, 389–403.

[16] V. Slavov, S. Dimova, Phase-field versus level set method for 2D dendritic growth, *Numerical Methods and Applications, Springer*, 2007, 717–725.

[17] J. Shen, X. Yang, Energy stable schemes for Cahn-Hilliard phase-field model of two-phase incompressible flows, *Chin. Annals of Mathematics*, Vol. 31B(5), 2010, 743–758.

[18] P. P. Valko, J. Abate, Comparison of sequence accelerators for the Gaver method of numerical Laplace transform inversion, *Computers and Mathematics with Applications*, Vol. 48.3, 2004, 629–636.